Early to Rise

Early to Rise

A Suffolk Morning

HUGH BARRETT

Foreword by Ronald Blythe
Drawings by Roderic Barrett

Farming Press

First published in 1967
Second paperback edition 1994
Reprinted 1995

ISBN 0 85236 273 0

A catalogue record for this book is available
from the British Library

Published by Farming Press Books
Wharfedale Road, Ipswich IP1 4LG, United Kingdom

Distributed in North America
by Diamond Farm Enterprises,
Box 537, Alexandria Bay, NY 13607, USA

Cover design by Andrew Thistlethwaite
Typeset by Galleon Typesetting
Printed and bound in Great Britain by Biddles Ltd,
Guildford and King's Lynn

Introduction

Ronald Blythe

IT is just over a quarter of a century since Hugh Barrett's delightful farm-student autobiography was first published and to myself and to many East Anglians it has remained one of the most truthful and unflinching views of our countryside during the last years of the great agricultural depression. Much has been written about those times but little with such intimacy and accuracy. They called it 'the coming down time' and here we have that farming collapse at its nadir – and with no one being aware that both the second agricultural revolution and a second world war (the two upheavals were of course linked) were in sight. The fascination of this book is its ability to present a moment of rural history as it appeared to a sixteen-year-old Quaker-bred lad who was neither looking back nor forward, but just being 'present'.

Hugh Barrett was taken on at Home Farm, a typically run-down situation in which fine men and horses struggled in a poverty which was common, and for which there was no answer other than a philosophical stoicism. He was set to traditional tasks by the Guv'nor and fed by Madam but left to make what he could of the strange mixture of splendid craftsmanship and economic muddle which surrounded him. His achievement is to give a sharp description of both with the recaptured vision of a boy. He sees everything, as a teenager does, but with the limited understanding of his years, so that his writing is filled with the surprises, absurdities, beauties and sadness of this passing-away world. He has apprenticed himself as a working pupil for five shillings a week to the Guv'nor, a testy man who, like God, sees everything. There is a memorable account of a fieldscape which is all weeds and rabbits, and of a village in decay. But as it is 1933 nothing is extraordinary. What is amazing is the vivid total recovery of this now mercifully vanished sight which, one should add, fails to be depressing because it is seen through such youthful eyes. In *Early to Rise* Hugh Barrett is standing on the headland of his own existence, gazing with a mixture of hope, amusement and fatalism at the row he has to plough.

One of the pleasures of this book is to have a full picture of how things were done on the farm sixty years ago. Craftsmanship and work methods are so expertly set out that they seem like a manual within the story itself. There is too the moodiness of youth, and Hugh Barrett is able to convey the helplessness of the farmworker during those hard times. The horsemen and stockmen of Home Farm speak the old language (notoriously difficult to write but authentically captured here) and are shown in all their economic precariousness. A single puff of displeasure from the Guv'nor and they would be finished. Finishing off plagues of rabbits, rats and fleas is another matter, and is described with zest.

This is the opening chapter of a writer-farmer's life, and one which is put together with a moving combination of tough realities and tenderness. *Early to Rise* is the kind of book which could be laid against some of today's rural history to measure its worth, yet its chief power is to prove how much we witness between childhood and all the decades which follow. For Hugh Barrett and for us who can now read him afresh, these are neither the bad old days nor the good old days, just those few months when he earned his first wage, and the larks sang, and the heavy tasks began to sort out the men from the boys.

vi

For Deirdre, our family and theirs

Chapter One

THERE is no exact record of the date, but it must have been in May. The Guv'nor said, 'It's a good start to learning farming – take a hoe and see how you get on in the beet.' The beet field – Park Field – was the largest on the farm. Ninety-two acres stretching from the valley lane to Park Wood, and from Horse Meadow to the main road. The beet seedlings were just through and still in the two- and four-leaf stage: small, fragile, intertwined and just not winning the race against weeds. I had been taught at agricultural college that to get the heaviest yields of sugar beet you need to finish up with something over thirty thousand plants to the acre. You begin – or in the days before monogerm seed had been thought of, you began – with maybe twenty times as many, because beet has a multiple germ seed with from two to perhaps five plants growing from it. And the drills of those days did not accurately space the seeds as they went into the ground but dropped them in an even flow. The art of the hand hoer was first, with as few strokes as possible, to disentangle the close and twisted stems and then leave the singled plant free of weeds and at the correct distance from its next neighbours.

I have not yet succeeded in a satisfactory estimate of the minimum number of individual hoe movements needed to 'single' an acre of clean crop: in a foul crop it must run into a hundred thousand or more. This crop was not clean. There was fat hen, charlock – *carlicks* we called them, winter weed, warlock, coltsfoot, wild mustard, spurrey and twitch, with a sprinkling of others: poverty weed, wiregrass, knotgrass. And the land was hard; each chop of the hoe jarred the wrists. Mercifully, the field had been drilled the short way, but even so the rows were over four hundred yards long and neither before nor since have I met longer ones. They stretched away past breakfast and 'bait' time, ended at dinner time by the wood, started back in the afternoon and finished at five. In the first two days I hoed precisely two rows a day – eight hundred yards – just there and back, and the rest of the field looking bigger each day, extending into an aching and bent-backed future.

To be sixteen years old and spend the first week of paid employment alone in a beet field as vast as that ninety-two acres was, maybe, a rough baptism, but it spelled out in unmistakable terms two facts. First, that my pupilage was a working one, and second, that even a chosen and desired occupation or profession is heavily compounded with elements of drudgery. A paying pupil would not have been set to work in this way: a little haymaking and harvesting perhaps, a lot of hunting and shooting and going to markets; never hoeing, for this was work for daymen and casuals, and in 1932 these were cheap and low in the farming hierarchy. The Guv'nor wanted these two facts impressed upon me early, and he succeeded. A back which screamed to be straightened for one week and which screamed if it was straight the next, was an effective way of doing it.

So for the first week I was alone but under the

2

Guv'nor's eye. Twice a day he drove his old Morris onto the headland and walked up the rows to where I was chopping and hacking. 'Getting along nicely, young man?' he'd ask. 'Back ache a bit? You've left a "double" there – don't want them.' And as he watched, my hoe would become even more inexpert and a plant selected for singling would be irreplaceably chopped out. It's a fact no one can single beet with someone looking over his shoulder at what he is doing – no, no matter how good he is.

By the end of the week I was clear of the headland and doing three rows a day, and, although it was never stated in so many words, I had passed the first test. I was accepted as a member of the working force at the Home Farm – the home of the Guv'nor and his family

– the main farm of the four which made up the estate: all hired land. The Home, Pantons Hall, Whitehouse and the Lodge Farm: in all a thousand acres mostly of poor sandy soil, intermixed with rough heath and noble woods which had somehow escaped the axe of the Great War. The hedges were tall and wide, the wooden five-barred gates inevitably hung upon a single hinge, the barn roofs leaked, and none of the buildings had smelt paint for a generation. But for me it was something like paradise; and to this day I can still only remember it in a romantic haze. Broken gates, rusty pails, old iron in the stackyard, ragweed on the meadows – all have a golden light on them.

Chapter Two

BEFORE I left school, father wanted me to become an economist. He admired Keynes and detested Churchill, whose period at the Treasury he believed to have caused more mischief than enough, in which he was probably right. But I doubt whether he had any very clear idea of what economists do. He felt the *country* needed a planned economy, but possibly also in his mind was that the *family* needed *its* economy put on a sound footing, too – and what better way than to have an economist in the family? The difficulty was that the chosen vessel had no head for arithmetic, and despite the urgency of the situation – we were pretty near broke – there was not the least chance of my ever achieving the necessary scholarship and scholarships which would take me to a place of higher academic learning. For which I am now grateful: very grateful. I might have become an agricultural economist.

So an academic career was out. What were the alternatives? At this distance I have no memory of what, if any, suggestions were made; but during the last year of school I had spent some months on the Aran Islands in Galway Bay where Robert Flaherty was making one of the finest documentaries ever made, *Man of Aran*. Here I lived out of doors, on or in the sea, went rabbiting with P.J. the hero of the film's son, got drunk on poteen, fractured my skull in a fall from a racehorse and decided that whatever else I would never live the life of a townsman. P.J. taught me how to insert a well-thorned bramble down into the deep cracks of rocks where the local rabbits hid – there was no soil for burrows – and twist the bramble round and round until it was so firmly wound into the fur of the animal it could be drawn up to the surface and knocked on the head. He tried to teach me how to throw stones accurately underarm and regarded my overarm – the normal for English boys – as both funny and useless. By comparison it was; he could knock out a running rabbit at thirty yards with a six-ounce stone: I couldn't hit a sitter at half the distance. P.J. also tried to teach me where my sober limit was in relation to potations of poteen. The difficulty here was that one had to exceed the limit before one knew one had arrived at it and the value of the lesson was lost. Besides, P.J. could never be relied on to keep count and was thirstier and harder headed than I: two factors which cancelled each other out. But it was another step in education.

Anyway, how finally it was decided that I would be a farmer no one knows: maybe it was just an accident of fate, of which Father approved as a second and more practical choice. It just happened. Leaving school abruptly, I went to an agricultural college. The less said about this the better: though to this day I am not sure whether I was thrown out because my fees weren't paid or because I was discovered one night by the Principal in the laundry drying room with a female student and a bottle. He might have overlooked this innocent escapade, and it *was* innocent, but unfortunately the lass was the daughter of a member of his staff and the bottle was from his cellar. The combination was too much and he refused to listen to reason. So, with the rudiments of dairy hygiene, double-entry book-keeping, and such practical knowledge as I had acquired of an afternoon grooming show cattle, shoeing horses (one shoe only) sheep shearing (one and a half sheep) and pruning blackcurrants, my term and a half came to an abrupt end. In self-defence I might claim I was over-young to be thrown among the much older and harder-bitten sons of farmers of the institution, that I was led astray. There is some truth in it, but not enough to compel respect. I now see, and indeed I saw at the time, that Authority had no option but to sling me out; but it was a pity none the less, for I was learning fast, and if at the same time the living was fast too, well, it was all of a piece, which is what life should be.

At sixteen, dramatic and unforeseen changes for the worse are not gloomily coloured by much thought of how they will affect the future. There is an immediate black despair, a sense of having lost all — but not for long. If my hurried departure from college and the knowledge that there were to be no more nights in the laundry left a scar, it was a small one. And there were advantages. For one thing, from henceforward I could choose whether to eat mutton or not. At college there was no choice: it was mutton or starvation — and for this reason. Senior students who showed an aptitude for any particular branch of farming or horticulture were privileged to acquire the status of honorary foremen. They helped the specialist instructors and when the instructors were absent took a certain amount of responsibility for running the department: it might be the milking herd or the piggery, the glass houses or, as in the case relevant to this episode, the flock of

Southdown ewes. The instructor shepherd was laid up for the first week of term: the cause — which is not relevant — was reliably thought to be the results of an over-indulgence in alcohol or amatory passions — or more probably both. Students are liable to think such things. The student shepherd was fairly experienced and he was competent enough, until one afternoon he came into the pasture to find that his sheep had strayed and were busy stuffing themselves on a particularly succulent young growth of clover next door. He knew — everyone is taught this — that although pigs are happy in clover, sheep (and other ruminants) are liable to be severely upset if they overdo the stuff. If they are not introduced to young clover gently — a few minutes a day to begin with — they may get hoven or bloat. The green material ferments inside, produces gas, and in a very short time the animal begins to expand. A little longer and it is — in a lopsided fashion — blown up and tight as a drum, the skin on the near side being pushed up higher than the animal's back. In a classic case of bloat in sheep the animal in an agony of discomfort lies down and wriggles and twists until it gets all four feet in the air and is helpless. The processes of fermentation go on until the expanded stomach pushes forward against the lungs and heart and the poor beast dies. If caught in an early stage, a drench — in those days it would likely have been a tablespoon of turpentine along with some linseed oil — poured down its throat would do the trick, but in the later stages the cure is more drastic and less certain — the knife. The aim is to pierce the rumen and let off the gas, thus easing pressure on the other vital organs. Now, to find the correct spot — and it is the same in cattle — you must find the centre of the triangle formed between the hip-bone, the lower edge of the back-bone and the last rib on the near side. Put in the knife at an angle to avoid the kidney, pierce the rumen and the gas will rush out and – unless it dies from infection – the animal will recover. It is a simple enough matter to demonstrate on a thin crone of a shorn ewe just where the puncture must be made: on a fat, full-fleeced animal distended with wind it is not so simple. These were in the last stages of bloat and whether our student knifed too little or too much, or on the wrong side or otherwise in the wrong places, I don't know. What I and some eighty other students soon discovered was that the college refrigerators were crammed with the rapidly butchered carcasses of the flock and, from that day until some time after I had gone and a spontaneous revolt broke out and put an end to it, it was mutton for luncheon, tea and supper – a diet which left me with a distaste for mutton in any form for many years.

My qualifications for taking any sort of job in farming were small, and at that time – the early thirties – with unemployment everywhere, the number of farmers looking for additions to the pay-roll was small too. I was lucky to find one who was not only willing for me to live in and learn as I went along but would pay me as well: five shillings a week – enough to keep me in clothes, with some to spare. Skilled men got about thirty shillings a week.

Chapter Three

HOME FARM lay in a shallow dip down a lane, half a mile from the main road. There were two 'tied' cottages, single storey thatched dwellings with brick-faced, clay-lump walls facing the lane, where the second and third horsemen lived with their families. Farther down, another pair of cottages where two daymen lived, and then the lane ended at the farm gate, widening out into the yard. On the left as you entered, end-on to the yard, a corrugated iron cowshed; next to it, a workshop and a wide alleyway to the thatched barn which, with its double doors wide open on both sides, gave an unexpected view of the fields behind. Next to the barn, the stables.

The long red brick and tile stable building, with the hay-loft above, was really the heart of the farm. It was here that the Guv'nor came each morning to give his orders for the day. At the side of the stables, the walled horse-yard, with a great iron drinking trough, roofed over and fitted out with hay-racks. Beyond this, the engine shed, and another workshop, and then a wide grassy area in front of the house itself. So these buildings and the house made a more or less continuous line down the left of the yard. On the right of the yard roadway were the engines and tackle for the threshing outfits – four or five of them, because the Guv'nor was a contractor as well as a farmer. They stood there, the

11

drums and chaff-cutters sheeted down and the engines, black and rusty, open to the air, under the line of oak-trees which stood between the yard and Horse Meadow. At the end of the yard and level with the house, the pond – a quarter-acre stretch of water, shallow at the edge, but deep enough to swim a horse in at the far side: inhabited by persecuted moorhens, a few ducks and a pair of geese which, having escaped the knife because they were too small one Christmas past, had somehow lived on to an age made safe by accumulated years and toughness.

Besides providing water for the horse meadow and a useful reserve when the wells were drying, the pond had another use. During long dry spells wagon and tumbril wheels would sometimes get shaky; spokes would rattle in the nave and the tyres would get loose from the felloes, so the carts would be jacked up and the wheels rolled down the lane and into the pond. Here they would soak for a couple of days before being put back on freshly greased arms. The wood swollen with water would be tight and safe for another season.

Home Farm was 'one ended'. Beyond the garden at the back of the house the woods which joined it belonged to another estate. They rose up steeply, oaks and ash, with holly and a thick undergrowth of hazel, sheltering the house and garden from the north-east. The house itself, stud and plaster, had once been coloured reddish brown, and then cream, and perhaps later a pink shade; but now it was a warm indeterminate colour, patchy, stained with green on one corner where a faulty gutter overflowed, and with bits of plaster bulging and in places fallen away. The windows, once white, were almost paintless. Yet despite this it had an air of snugness, of being warm and lived in, and it didn't seem to matter that the garden was untidy, and the corrugated lean-to which served as a dairy at the back was rusty red. The outside of the house was of course the landlord's responsibility. He had no money for repairs: the Guv'nor wasn't going to do the landlord's work and, anyway, he hadn't got money for frippery like paint either.

In most East Anglian farmhouses the front door is never used except by visitors from town who don't know any better. Home Farm was unusual in that its front door, which faced the yard, was used by everyone. It was protected by a small brick-floored porch with side seats, and the door itself stood open most of the year, showing a passage off which were the kitchen, dining room and the drawing room, the latter scarcely ever used except at Christmas. It wasn't an ancient house – probably late seventeenth century – but the mud scraped from generations of boots had built up the garden so that the walls seemed sunk in the ground. It had shrugged itself down into a comfortable old age. The woods behind, the great oak on the bit of green in front, the splintered willow by the pond, all contributed to make an atmosphere which must have remained unchanged for generations. For me it was a case of always has been and always will be. That it could ever have been different – that those giant oaks had ever been saplings, or the buildings new and painted and without corrugated iron additions, was beyond imagining.

After the initial back-breaking week of solitary hoeing, I soon slipped into the routine of the farm life: it fitted

13

me like a glove. Luckily I had always been easy to get out of bed, so the early rising was no hardship. What was more difficult to get used to was the early to bed rule. It is almost impossible to believe; but the whole family, the Guv'nor and 'Madam' (as she was called by everyone) and their family of four, ranging from twenty-one down to fifteen, all went to bed when it was dark in summer-time and never later than eight o'clock in the winter. More often, it was seven-thirty. I didn't complain, and I never heard any of the family complain about it either: it was accepted as the natural thing. Not that there would have been much to do had we stayed up. No wireless – a very ancient gramophone and five or six records provided the only music I ever heard there – and maybe a score of books in the drawing room. I was quite openly discouraged by Madam from reading these. 'I don't think you would like them, Hugh,' she said, and then added: 'They are not really suitable for young people'. Nor, indeed, in her younger days were they thought to be suitable reading for any nice person of any age; for these volumes, handsomely bound and acquired from heaven knows what farm sale, were by Ouida! And I enjoyed them!

My bedroom was at the north end of the house, with one window looking east to catch the first signs of dawn and the other on the west facing the yard and buildings. Lying in bed, I could hear the cock pheasants going up to roost in the wood behind the house and the night movements from the horse-yard: the rustle of hay being pulled from the racks and, on still nights, the steady 'chump chump chump' of feeding horses. The room had one disadvantage. That end of the house was next to the lean-to woodshed, and under the piled logs rats had a regular road through the outer wall, up the studs in the plaster, and from there into the spaces between floors and ceilings. There were rat holes in every room, but mine had most. Two under the chest of drawers, one by the door, one at the corner of the fireplace, and two between floor and wall near the head of my bed, and another on the edge of a beam where ceiling and wall joined. Most of them had been covered with tin: boot-polish tin-lids were nailed all round, but new holes were always in process of being gnawed.

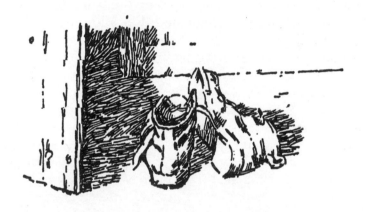

As dusk fell, the house would begin to sound with little tentative scuffling noises. Small rustles, a gentle scratching. You could hear one on one side of the wall and another on the other. The sounds would gradually get closer to each other, and then – usually, it seemed, in the wall behind my head – the two would meet,

15

there'd be a scuffle, a shrill squeak, and the night's games were on. Behind every wall, over the ceiling and under the floor, big rats and little rats would be racing up and down, fighting, dragging bits of wood and bits of tin along narrow passages, playing football, copulating, gossiping, playing follow-my-leader, catch-as-catch-can, and (if there were a couple of open holes in the floor) last-across. Sometimes the yard cat would steal into the woodshed and interrupt the merrymaking. There would be a scrabble and a scream, a mad rush in all directions, and, for ten minutes, absolute silence. Then it would begin all over again. One got used to it, and if in the night the activity got to such a pitch that I woke, a heavy boot slung in the general direction of the row quietened things long enough for sleep to come again.

Perhaps that year was a bad one for rats. The rise and fall of local rat populations does seem to go in cycles — or it did in the days before Warfarin and the new, deadlier poisons came on the market. Anyway, it led to trouble. We were all pretty fed up with them. They had got bold — or numerous enough even to slip across the dining room while we were at meals, which was a bit too much. It happened that one day while the Guv'nor was out two chaps turned up and offered to clear the house and outbuildings for ten bob. Madam agreed. They had a couple of rough terriers and a box of ferrets, and an air of knowing all about rats and their ways. They started in the garage, worked their way via the dairy and the woodshed, where the terriers had a brisk ten minutes catching five full grown rats and a score or more young ones, and then to the house. This is where the ferrets came in. Ferrets are not lovely things at any time. These were great yellow-brown polecats and savage. The lid of the box was opened and they were dragged out, blinking their pink eyes in the light, and thrust into holes in the outer walls of the house. Two at the corner of the kitchen, two by the front door and one by the back. The men and dogs took up strategic positions in the woodshed and at another great main drain of a hole by the dairy. For a few minutes there was a great carry-on under the floors downstairs: two or three rats were snapped up as they escaped by the dairy and a few more were served the same way in the woodshed. Then the interior scufflings moved up the walls as the ferrets, having chased the vermin from the ground floors, moved up in pursuit. More noises from the bedroom areas: a few terrified squeaks, and three young rats were observed in the gutters outside, but they found their way back into the house.

All that morning the ratcatchers waited but although the noises of the chase inside the house went on, not a whisker was seen outside. Neither of rat, nor – and this was the vital matter – of ferrets either. By mid after-noon all thought of rat catching had been given up, and the aim was to recapture the ferrets before dark-ness fell. A rabbit was gutted and put enticingly near one hole; the ferrets' box was left open, warm and inviting, near another; but both were ignored. At five o'clock, and without saying farewell (but with the ten bob which they had prudently extracted from Madam during dinner-time), the catchers left. And *we* were left with four ugly-natured ferrets and a scarcely altered rat population. When he got home the Guv'nor was not pleased, and by next morning he was furious, for the hunt in the walls had gone on all night. The patter of

17

feet, the sudden screams, the chases, thumps and rattles were worse than they had ever been. However, during the dinner hour that day, the warrener (there were more than enough rabbits on the estate to keep one working full time) came to the door to say he had just caught a ferret in a rat trap at the bottom of the garden, and in the afternoon the back'us boy cornered another in the dairy. That night the rats seemed quieter. Obviously the ferrets had frightened them away and we thought the uncaptured pair had themselves gone off to the woods or the buildings or, as the Guv'nor hinted with a sly look at Madam, to the fowlhouse on the Horse Meadow: Madam's pin money came from the egg sales. So we slept quiet for a couple of nights.

Unfortunately the story did not end there. Two days later, a faint but nasty smell centred somewhere in the kitchen began to ooze through the house – a smell of unparalleled nastiness. It grew in strength and pungency. Cooking there became impossible and Madam transferred to the dairy with an oilstove. Next day the stench was so strong in the dining room we had to eat in the drawing room, something which I reckon had never been done before, except maybe mince pies at Christmas – and next day even the drawing room was reeking. Dead rat in warm weather is powerful: dead ferret – or, more likely, two dead ferrets – raises the pong to the power of nausea. I have never, before nor since, smelt such a corruption. But, strange to say, I think the remaining rats disliked it too: anyway, as, at the end of a long week, the smell died away, leaving only suggestive reminders in cupboards and closed places, we found the rats had gone. Though whether they had died or walked out no one could say.

18

Chapter Four

GETTING up in the morning, as I have said, was not hard for me. Even as a small boy I liked being about before the human world was moving, before the morning has been touched by people. Even on the clearest summer morning the air is different, unused, and a little mysterious, and one senses a life which, like the sea, moves in its own unceasing secret fashion. A couple of hours after dawn and it's all workaday once more, familiar and some of the magic gone. On winter mornings the blankets did pull a bit. The Guv'nor would shout up the stairs that it was time to get up. One lay in bed for a few moments looking for light at the window, but five thirty was too soon for even a tremble on the eastern horizon. Light a candle, struggle into breeches, shirt, jersey, and tumble downstairs to the kitchen where the Guv'nor was sitting by the blazed up kindling sticks in the grate and the kettle steaming on the bars. The Guv'nor never said much at any time, but before breakfast one syllable at a time was enough: 'tea' – and he poured it out, adding sugar from a dessert spoon. He opened the crock which stood ready on the table: 'Bun ?' – and we ate two good hard Suffolk rock buns. This by the light of the fire and a single candle: just enough to make warm yellow patches on the walls and catch a shine on the brown painted settle and beams; the rest faded into sombre shadow.

It was no good asking the Guv'nor what was scheduled for the day's work ahead at this time. He wouldn't say. At ten to six we finished the second cup and the second rock bun, tapped the barometer, and went out across the yard to the stable where for an hour or more George the head horseman had been at work feeding and grooming, and the under-horsemen were ready to harness up. The Guv'nor and George had a quiet word or two together while the rest of us stood waiting on them and their decisions, and the horses blew out the last grains of oats from the more abundant chaff in the mangers. Then, having organized every-thing to their liking, the Guv'nor would disappear towards the barn where the daymen would get their orders direct from him, and George relayed ours. He began with his second in command – his brother Willy – and went on down in order of hierarchical impor-tance to third, fourth and fifth horsemen, telling each one what he was to do and the order in which the jobs must be done. A load of hay from the stackyard into the horse-yard; mangolds for the cowshed; a pair of horses to be shod by the village blacksmith (this was a job for me); two pairs to plough; a pair for the beet-lifting, and two in tumbrils for beet-carting. George never made a mistake: he, or he and the Guv'nor between them, could reckon up to the minute how long each job should take, making automatic adjustments for the different men and the different horses. They knew Joe and Duke would shift more beet in an hour than Joe and Diamond, and that Willy and Blossom would do more than anyone. These inborn work-rates for man and beast were all calculated but not, I think, unduly taken advantage of. If only because, while George and the Guv'nor knew, the rest of us *knew* they knew, and things had to be fair.

The Home stable had ties for fourteen horses and when I was there it was full of pure-bred Suffolks with traditional Suffolk names. George's pair were Blossom, the smallest mare in the stable and the most willing puller I've ever met with, and Bowler, a gelding with unusually good feet. He was a favourite for beet-hoeing because he never walked on the rows. Willy's pair were mixed, too: a tall gelding called Captain and a biggish mare, Matchett, with an almost flaxen mane and tail. Third horseman Walter had Diamond, with a star on her nose, and Duke, a gaunt animal of great size and reputed to be twenty years old. Then there were two Boxers – Big Boxer and Little Boxer – Major, Kitty, Gypsy, and Ginger – a mountain of a horse who, as the men said, 'came off the streets' and was inclined to be mangey. Ginger had pulled a coal cart at the docks, and was good in traffic but hopeless in any job like horse-hoeing, because he floundered all over the place and put his ugly great feet on the seedlings. He was usually left for the odd jobs round the yards and was everyone's unfavourite.

Nowadays the stable is empty. Matchett survived

21

until 1959, I think – l saw her last about then, standing alone and forlorn in a corner of Horse Meadow, flaxen tail to wind, her head hanging, her lower lip drooping, her ribs and hip bones visible beneath the skin: a sad picture, as though she had forgotten the time when the meadow was alive with good companions, and didn't want to remember.

But in the 'thirties the stables were the centre, the powerhouse of the farm. I suppose there were seven or eight hundred acres of arable land, and most of it had to be ploughed, harrowed, drilled, rolled and harvested with horse-drawn implements nearly every year. The one tractor – an International 10/20 – was used for heavy cultivating, and neither the tractor nor its driver were thought much of by the horse people. The tractor driver started work alone in the morning and worked all day by himself – a man apart, cut off from his fellows by the nature of the machine and the things it could do and horses could not, and the things it could *not* do which the horses could. These were the days of the argument which went on for ten years or more: do tractors *pan* the land more than horses? We had no doubts!

For the first few weeks at Home Farm I worked round the buildings or on the beet field at the end of the lane: either helping out the yardman, mixing up the pig grub, grinding corn and feeding, or with the back'us boy, doing odd-job carting and cleaning up the cowshed. It took that time to learn my way about, to find where everything was kept: which bin had oats in it, in which corner of the granary to put the brooms, where the harness oil was hidden or the big wrenches used on the threshing tackle. It was all complicated for me by not knowing the words, or the pronunciation of words for things. I didn't know a dutfin was a bridle; that a brawcher or broatche was another word for springel (with a soft 'g'), a peg used by thatchers; or that a wanty was the band from shaft to shaft under the horse's belly, which prevented the tumbril from tipping up when the back was heavier than the front.

For the odd jobs, Ginger was the horse. He was very tall, and I was undersized and short. Moreover, Ginger was old and knew more than I about how a horse should be harnessed: he did not approve of amateurs and showed his disapproval by holding his head as high as he could when I offered the collar up to his nose. A good mannered horse will drop his head so that the collar can be lodged on his nose, and then raise it so that with a helping shove it slips neatly over the head

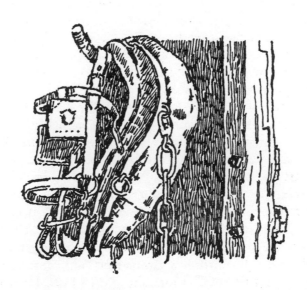

and is then revolved a half turn and settled on the shoulders. Finding I could not reach his stuck up nose from the floor, I hit on the idea of raising myself by standing in the manger and trying the collar from there. Ginger promptly dropped his head between his knees. When I got down, up went his head again. It was a game that might have gone on for an hour, but Georgy – he was called Georgy to distinguish him from George the head horseman – came into the stable, took the collar from me, walked up to Ginger and said 'Ho'd up, you o'd Davil' – and the horse offered his head, the collar slipped on, and I had learned a lesson. Horses – and for that matter, dogs, cattle, and men – dislike being messed about by people who don't know their job. Georgy was my age, but he had the authority which knowing how to do a thing properly gives a man: he had been at it since fourteen and had probably never had to think about how to harness a horse – he'd been brought up by a horseman father and grandfather, and been in and out of stables from the time he could walk and maybe before that.

After the collar, the saddle. I was foxed here to begin with, too, because it was never called a saddle, but a pad. This of course is what it is – a pad with a wooden frame atop with the channel for the chain which supports the weight of the tumbril. The pads were hung at the back of the stable, each one complete with britchens or breechens, the heavy leather strapping which prevents the cart over-running the horse on a downhill slope, and into which the horse backs. They were heavy, and it took a deal of effort to sling them neatly on a big horse without the girth getting under the pad and the whole lot sliding off again. Horses hate

24

things slipping from their backs. Ginger turned his ugly head and looked at me with an expression of utter contempt when this happened. Georgy might have, but he didn't. He had a way with animals, and with people too, which by the time he was forty had brought him to near the top of the business of showing cattle — but that was still a long way off, and for the time he was just the back'us boy, my mentor and good friend.

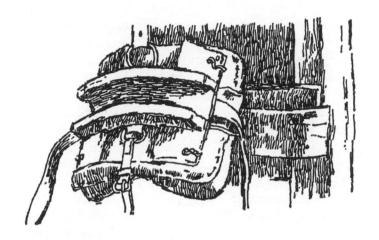

After the pad and britchens, the hames or seals had to go on the collar. These are the two curved wooden or iron pieces which go round the outside of the leather of the collar, are joined at the base by a short thong, and near the top by a top latch or top lash, a specially strong leather thong cut from the hide of a bull's neck. A yard in length and quite thin, it had to be threaded through a hole in one hame and then turned round the other and finished in a hitch which would not come undone:

25

important, since the hames carry the chains or hooks by which the horsepower is transmitted to the cart or implement. Nothing looks sillier than a horse standing in a cart with the hames hanging from the shafts – and it happened to me, of course. Top latches were rather personal pieces of equipment. Each horseman had his own, and they were often the cause of hard words. 'Yar hed moi toplatch' – 'That ar hen't – this 'ere's un a' had offen George two month agoo.' – 'That yow didn't: his'n was bruk and had a knot in it: that ther's mine.' Anyway, there was always a shortage of good top latches, and I think the men used to keep them in their dinner bags at night. I could never find one that wasn't old and stiff and knotted, and would break if twisted the wrong way round the hames.

Strictly speaking, harness should have been in sets: one set for each horse of the simple plough gear – dutfin, collar, backstrap, and plough chains – and a set of thil or filler gear – the heavier harness for cart and wagon work. But the Home harness had been collected in odd lots and bits and pieces from sales all over Suffolk and Essex. No piece really belonged to its fellow, and only over the years had this or that piece come to be regarded as the piece for this or that horse: there was still room for dispute. There were two kinds of hames or seals: plough hames were fitted with hooks, so that the plough chains could be adjusted link by link; whereas the thil gear or cart hames had short chains permanently attached. Whenever I wanted cart hames, all I could find were plough hames. It was all very confusing. The harness was mostly in poor repair too. One could never be sure that an extra pull on a girth wouldn't snap it at the buckle; but at least we were not so badly off as the miserable Scots farmer two parishes away who drove his horses in cart or wagon shafts without any britchens at all. There was some argument locally whether this was because he couldn't afford them, or because he never wanted his horses to stop — the cart, unchecked by britchens, would of course bump into the horses' hindquarters and 'ke'p them a goen'.

Chapter Five

GEORGY may have been my age, but he was much more mature and wise. As we went about together, he passed on to me in a quiet way a great deal of the farm lore, laws and old saws which he and everyone else there had been brought up on, so that gradually I lost all sense of being a stranger or an outsider. I knew where things were, what they were called, and if at first there were only a very few jobs I could do without advice or physical help, the list was growing all the time: I was finding my place. It was only as time went on that I realised how ill-defined that place was. In fact, I was the odd fish, the only person in the farm hierarchy who was not fitted into a pattern established by long precedent. Not so strange, really, since there had never been a pupil on the estate before me. I think even the Guv'nor was uncertain whether it was quite right, since I lived in the house, for me to muck out the pigs along with Georgy. Living in his house, in the eyes of the men, I automatically acquired some of the status of the family. In the eyes of the Guv'nor, because I worked for him, I had some of the status of his lowest servant. But the edges were blurred, and it was due to all their innate decency and kindness that only rarely did I feel other than at home either indoors, or out of doors with the men.

Everyone else knew exactly where they stood: this

was an authoritarian society and no democratic non-sense from the Guv'nor. He was the pinnacle of power, and he deserved to be. He knew more than we did about the land, about markets and about livestock, and with a thousand acres at his command he was a man of importance in the parish and beyond. He may not have been a big man – no more than five foot eight – and his voice, as with so many Suffolk farmers, was high pitched and squeaky, but when he spoke you listened and obeyed – promptly. He couldn't bear to see people with their hands in their pockets. In fact it infuriated him. 'Hands cold?' he'd shout, 'I must find something for you to do, or' – and his voice fairly cracked with rage – 'perhaps you'd like to warm y'self indoors at the fire?' This was a fearful jibe. It hinted that perhaps one might be better fitted for an indoors job – a job in an office, where, according to him, 'you can earn more money and polish the seat of your breeches while you're doing it'. Farmers then, even more than now, despised pen-pushers, clerks and salesmen – and business-men, too, unless they happened to be particularly successful or knowledgeable about farming. Really, the world was split into two main divisions: those who farmed or, like auctioneers and millers, were intimately bound up with agriculture; and those who were outside, who earned their cash in mysterious ways involving sharp practice and financial juggling beyond belief. There were, of course, divisions within these main lines of demarcation: owner-occupiers; tenant farmers and smallholders; business, clergy, and, quite apart, the gentry.

George, the head horseman, was first man. The Guv'nor openly asked his opinion about the state of the land: would Bottom Piece harrow down, or would it be better left till another day: how much seed would he want put ready for drilling the Hicks: and, naturally, all questions directly relating to horse health or implements would be referred to him. But equally, all the men would go to George for advice and support: even the tractor driver, who normally kept himself to himself, looked to George when he was in difficulties. George was a small man but wiry, very quiet and soft-spoken, yet his voice with animals had the unmistakable tone of authority. There was one day, a Monday morning, when the horses were standing fresh in the stable after the week-end rest, ready to leave for the fields. Half of them were already harnessed and untied, and about to be led across the yard, when a pony mare belonging to one of the children trotted into the stable. Her bright little hooves went pank pank pank on the pammets, and for some reason this sent the Suffolks into a state of near hysteria. Within a couple of seconds the whole stable was a riot of tangled reins, broken harness and flying hooves, with the pony mixed up somewhere in the middle of them squealing with fear and excitement. You couldn't see her for the greater bulk of the carthorses, and they couldn't see her either, because she scarcely reached their bellies. It was frightening.

I bolted for the door; one of the horsemen shinned up the wall-ladder into the hay loft; another took a running dive into the chaff-house; and Walter, who had hung on to his pair until they became unmanageable and were dragging him under the flying heels of Big Boxer, jumped into the open corn hutch. George, who had been out in the yard greasing a cart-wheel, heard the row, the stamping, the squealing and the shouting, and came at the run. First he *shut* the stable door, and then walked quietly right into the middle of the mêlée, grabbed the pony mare by jaw and forelock, and, talking quietly all the time, led her out into the yard. Then back into the stable again with the Suffolks still milling and kicking. He spoke first, and sharply, to his own pair: 'Bowler, standstill; Blossom, steady now, git in there and standstill.' 'Standstill' is a key word. They quietened and stood, and George went on, singling out the most obedient first: 'Captain, git you back, woa, woa hoss, stand. . . .'

And then the rest of us came out from our retreats with rather red faces to face him — and later the Guv'nor and his music. It was rough, and higher pitched than I'd heard. 'Anybody hurt?' The Guv'nor had a way of always laying emphasis on the 'body': 'Any*body* hurt?' We shuffled our feet and murmured 'No'.

'Well, who let the pony mare out? Who left the cart-stable door open? Come along, George, what's the meaning of this mess?' And he looked round at the broken harness on the floor, the smashed broom handle, the collar with the stuffing ripped out of it, and the blood which George was mopping up on Diamond's hind leg. None of us chaps said a thing, and then George's quiet, almost soothing voice answered: 'I think, Guv'nor — though, mind you, I don't know fer sartain, I think that there pony mare is a comen on song, and I reckon she've kicked har door open and come round heah a looken fur suthen ter ride her.' He hesitated for a moment, and then added: 'You recollect I did happen to mention as how the sneck on har door was bruk last week, and wanted a nail or suthen to hold

31

it safe.' The Guv'nor didn't bother to acknowledge the truth of the statement: he just said 'Hah', and then 'Hum', and then, looking keenly at George as if to suggest this was not the proper time to mention such a thing, said: 'Well, get you along together, get the mess cleared up, and see Diamond doesn't go lame neither,' and off he went. With the Guv'nor out of earshot the chaps relaxed. 'He din't take that too bad,' said George, and the others agreed – more or less – Walter adding: 'If his hid had bin where mine damn nearly were when old Ginger let fly, he wouldn't have nothen to put his cap on!' And another put in: 'Hey, Walter, if you'd a bin kicked where I damn near was, you wouldn't be arter botheren the gels no more, neither!' We were back in the bawdy good comradeship of the normal early morning.

Chapter Six

O F all the men George was the best ploughman: he could set out a 'top' over the brow of a hilly field which would be straight as a gun barrel. His drilling was near perfection – so near that it was hard to find the 'wheelings' to follow when it came to horse-hoeing the root crops. Otherwise his strength lay in the broad field of farming wisdom: he was no specialist apart from his horses. His brother Willy (that's how he was christened) was a much bigger man, though with the family quiet speech. He never claimed to be the skilled man his brother was: good, yes, but not superb. But he had something George hadn't and that was the art of stacking. He could make boat-ended, or square ended, or round stacks. He knew the size of the fields, he would estimate the crop, and then, if the Guv'nor wanted it that way, he would set out his stack bottom so that the last sheaf on the field just fitted the last gap on the ridge of the stack roof. George admitted that this was 'afore my time', meaning it was something he couldn't do. The two brothers liked working together. They rarely spoke as they worked, but I had the feeling they were in closest touch the whole time: speech was not needed.

Willy was second horseman, but he was not really second in the hierarchy. This would have to be shared by several men – the specialists. Harry, the young shepherd, was not old enough to qualify: at eighteen he showed all the signs of being a born shepherd – or he would not have been in charge of 250 good Suffolk ewes – but he was still 'the boy Harry', though the men already sensed, I believe, that he was a man apart. He, like his brother Georgy, went to the top of his profession in due course, though on other farms.

I reckon the Guv'nor would have rated Alby second man. He was the senior of the threshing tackle chaps, an engine driver who could make a seven-ton threshing engine 'jump a ditch like a steeplechaser'. That man ate coal and breathed steam and probably earned more for the Guv'nor than any five other men. He also did pretty fairly for himself – threshing chaps rate high on the tipping list – and I've heard tell that when the Guv'nor was in deeper water than usual, Alby offered to lend him a thousand pounds – which in 1932 or '33 was a hatful of money.

Alby was tiny. He perched up on his engine like a bird, twirling the low-geared steering wheel, and judging his speeds and distances to the inch. He could draw the train of threshing machine (always called the 'drum'), elevator, baler (a four-ton R.S.J. wiretyingmachine), and finally, maybe a chaff-cutter and water cart as well, across narrow bridges, through narrower gateways, across boggy stackyards, and down between two rows of stacks with less fuss than a girl pushing a pram on the highroad. I loved the sound of those engines. The steady chchch-chchc chchchchc chchchch as she came along the road: the slowing down as she approached the gate – a whisper of escaping steam: and then, as Alby gently hit the release valve with the palm of his hand, she would give a couple of slow chuuuuf-chuuuufs; and then, when everything was lined up and Alby hit her hard, she would go ahead with governor balls spinning and smoke pouring from the funnel into the yard. It was a fine sight.

Contact between the threshing men and the farm chaps was only intermittent. They spent their weekends in the village, but the rest of the week they were in more distant places. Between them they covered an area of several hundred square miles, and knew more about the farmers and their crops and the gossip than anyone else. Not only did they talk to the men belonging to the farms where they were threshing, but to the odd bodies who always turned up when there was a chance of a day's work in the stackyard: so they knew a good deal, and through them the Guv'nor did, too. They knew whose corn was running well, whose missus was in the family way again, which father's sons were wild'uns, and whose worked 'harder than he do hisself'.

After Alby and the cowman and the man who did the wholesale greengrocery round into town every day – for the Home Farm grew acres of cabbages and cauliflowers and turnips and crops for the shops – there was the ruck of the rest of the men. Horsemen, milkroundsman, day-men – the chaps who could turn their hands to a lot of jobs, but who had no status worth the mention. The cowman must have had some importance, but he was a man who kept himself to himself, liked working alone, rarely spoke, and seemed content only when it was milking time and he was squatting on a milking stool with his greasy cap thrust up into the flank of a cow. There was no milking machine, and the Guv'nor drafted anyone who could milk into the cowshed to help out. And, of course, everyone bar the horsemen and the specialists was supposed to be able to milk at a pinch.

Hygiene was perhaps not the strongest point in the

35

dairy or the cowshed. In fact, if you had been foolish enough to ask the cowman what hygiene was, I doubt whether he would have understood what you were talking about. The cowshed was a long corrugated iron building with two ranks of cows at each side and a wide passage down the middle: wide enough to get a horse and cart along for bedding up and mucking out. It had once been whitewashed – perhaps more than once – but the walls were thick with dung, the divisions between the cows splashed with it and greasy with the grease from the animals. It was old-fashioned, not very economical to run, but it smelt sweet with the scent of hay and mangolds and the breath of the cows, and I don't know that anyone ever complained about the milk being visibly dirty: after all, it was cooled and strained. I've never really had any passion for cows: I like them well enough when they are housed in a warm building with a good rough floor and not too much light to attract the flies in; but the modern sterile cowsheds, all concrete and steel stanchions, and smelling of chemical detergents, insecticides and sterilizing agents, are places that repel me. The milk produced there may be cleaner, more hygienic – it undoubtedly is – but they are neither cosy nor comfortable, and belong to the factory rather than the farm.

Mind you, the Home Farm milking standards were probably lower than they had any right to be, and I think the sanitary inspectors (or whatever the officials were called in those days) had made a few suggestions for improving the buildings. Had they seen the actual milking operations they might have made a few more – or dropped dead with shock. Even I was a bit startled to find that chaps drafted in from the fields – say, from sugar beeting – would settle down against a cow, take a teat in one hand and squeeze a thick squirt of milk into the palm and then do the same with the other, wiping the mixture of mud and milk off on their coat-tails. This served two uses: it cleaned those parts of the hands which closed on the teats and lubricated the palm to make the operation easier; in any case, it is horribly uncomfortable to milk with gritty hands and this was the quick way of avoiding it. By the end of milking the chaps got up from their stools with their hands showing a wide moist, pink band across the palm and fingers between the darker accumulation of dirt from a day's work in the fields. This 'wet hand' milking was actually stopped during my time on the estate, but the whole manner of goings on in that department has left me with a permanently cavalier attitude to honest dirt in honest food: perhaps it doesn't matter much, so long as it is eaten fresh.

Such concentrates as the cows got were home grown unless the Guv'nor happened on a cheap lot of stuff at market – a load of decorticated cotton cake, or linseed, or perhaps Indian gram, or Plate maize. They were mixed up along with the barley and oats and beans, and put through the mill by Georgy. This was a weekly job, and I often helped. The grinding mill itself stood in an annexe at the end of the barn under the granary, and the engine which drove it had a small shed to itself, with its belt drive coming through the shed wall, across the passage between, and through the millhouse wall. This meant that if one wanted to get to the pigs or the main barn doors one had to duck under the endless belt which whirred and slithered alarmingly four feet from the ground. Carrying buckets under this without spilling was not easy – or safe; but, although several chaps had had their caps knocked off, I don't remember anyone being hurt: there were no guards of any sort – this was long before such things were thought necessary. The engine was a vast, single cylinder, oil-fuelled monster, and it was a devil to start from cold. The routine was to turn on the fuel cock, and then revolve the seven-foot diameter flywheel a few turns, with the compression valve open to suck oil into the cylinder. Then the valve was closed and the flywheel had to be turned over against compression. It was hard and (I thought) dangerous work. One had to stand on the spokes of the wheel to get it to revolve and then, just as compression point was reached, give a bit of a bounce and jump clear. If it *did* fire, you not only jumped, but were thrown off. If it didn't, then the whole process had to be started again until it did. The heavy whump whump and a cloud of thick oily smoke from the chimney meant she was off and going good. Sometimes, instead of the engine firing on the down stroke, she'd fire on the up, and the man on the wheel, instead of being thrown clear, was thrown upwards towards the corrugated iron roof.

No one actually reached the roof that I know of, but from time to time we all had our knees knocked up to our chins. Anyway, as Georgy said: 'So long as you miss the rafters you 'ont take no hurt – th' old roof's that rotten you'd go straight through it.'

Once the engine had started going the wrong way – that is, anti-clockwise instead of clockwise – rather than stop it and start again, we simply put a twist in the belt and let it go on, and the mill revolved in the correct direction.

Chapter Seven

GRINDING days were all right but I didn't like the dust. As we tipped the sacks into the hopper the dust rose, and as the mill bit into the grain it thickened. On a still day, within a few minutes it hung in the air adding more dust to the already thickly coated cobwebs festooning and hanging from the rafters. One's clothes whitened, hair took on a sudden frosted appearance, and footsteps were traced all over the floor. Georgy seemed not to mind, but I choked.

Perhaps another reason for my not liking grinding was that I showed up to such disadvantage when it came to carrying sacks down from the granary. The sacks were heavy, too heavy for my unaccustomed back and shoulders. It was not so much that I lacked the muscular strength as the knack, the ability to organize what strength I did have; and the sacks would never lie steady across my shoulders as they did for Georgy.

Georgy taught me the intricacies of agricultural weights and measures – a subject whose terms seem at first designed to confuse. For instance, grain yields were always spoken of in terms of 'quarters' or 'coombs' – a coomb being half a quarter. That was easy enough, but what was a coomb? The answer is a corn sack holding four bushels – in other words, a measurement of volume. So a quarter is two sacks of four bushels each. It sounds simple enough, and in the days when presumably corn was sold by volume it was simple. But no miller or merchant would think of buying corn by volume. He knows that the more husk and less meat there is in a sample of grain, the lighter and more worthless it is, and it takes up a bigger volume. So, although we used these terms of volume, weights were implied. Again, this would be simple if the weights were always the same, but they were not. A coomb of wheat had to weigh 18 stone; barley 16 stone; oats 12 stone; while peas and beans were weighed up in 19-stone sacks, and clover seed in 20 stones! To complicate things further, seed merchants bought clover seed at so much a bushel, but if the farmer bought seed from the merchant he paid so much a pound.

The Guv'nor carried a calculating machine in his head and never came unstuck in a bargain involving several different sets of terms; but it took me years before I could conclude a deal without the aid of pencil and paper. It's easier now that most things are bought and sold by the hundredweight, but I'll guarantee the present generation of educated farm workers, *and* their masters, are not half so good at mental arithmetic as their forebears were. Pigs were sold or quoted (as they are today) at so much a 'score' – twenty pounds live weight – but butchers – and in that part of Suffolk butchers often went round farms buying pigs and cattle – always calculated in stones, and to add confusion the butcher's stone was eight, instead of fourteen, pounds weight. Their stone was a deadweight figure, and probably originated in the fact that a liveweight 14 lb.-stone of pig would finish up as a stone of about eight pounds of pork. Anyway, it had more sense to it than appears at first sight. Actually, compared with years before the First World War, weights and measures were straightforward. As late as the late nineteenth century, a bushel of wheat would weigh different in different parts of the country: so you got the Gloucester Bushel of 62 lbs. and the Nantwich Bushel 75 lbs. and the Liverpool 70 lbs. Still, since corn didn't move about the country so much, I suppose it didn't matter.

Humping corn *down* the granary steps to the mill was harder than taking it up; there was something quite unnerving about standing at the top of the steps, which were wooden, steep and slippery, with eighteen stone of wheat on your shoulders pressing you downwards and outwards. The first time I tried, I leant backwards too far and the sack toppled me on to my backside. The second attempt failed in the middle, when the sack slipped sideways across my back, over the handrail, and fell fifteen feet – bursting on the muddy yard below. Keeping a sharp eye open for the Guv'nor, Georgy helped me scrape it up, called the fowls to scratch for what was left, and carefully put the split empty sack in the middle of a pile of good ones, where we hoped it would not be noticed. But it's a funny thing: the Guv'nor was not a 'creeper', he never soft-shoed round corners, one never saw him actually looking or probing into anything which on the face of it looked all right: yet, somehow or other, he had a knack of (as it were) *innocently* discovering the irregular.

A few days later, when Walter was pitching hay into the loft over the stables, he fractured his fork stale – its wooden shaft or handle. It wasn't broken through, just fractured. He put it in the corner where all the hayforks were standing, picked up another and got on with the job. A couple of minutes later in comes the Guv'nor, walks to the corner, picks up that fork and starts to help. Of course it bent and then broke with the first hoist. 'Do you know anything about this, Walter?' Walter stopped and scratched the back of his head, pushing his cap over his eyes. 'Well, sir, a'reckon tha's a poer bit of wood – tha' sorter bent 'a fust time I shuv'up a wodge.' 'Poor tool, or a damn clumsy man using it,' replied the Guv'nor, and then, spotting me looking down through the hole in the hayloft floor and wishing to include as many as possible in his annoyance, he said: 'And next time you split a corn sack, do you put it in the mending pile so I know about it.' 'The old bugger,' said Walter when he had gone. 'There's a dozen bloody forks stand in the corner and he hev ter chuse that 'un.'

What exercised my mind was how a man employing

just on fifty men scattered over a thousand acres managed so unerringly to know in detail the things we were all concerned, to greater or lesser degree, to prevent him from knowing. Since then I've learned that, although the Guv'nor had a particularly highly developed instinct in this direction, it is not all that uncommon. It is perhaps a matter of unceasing observation, of reading and recording in one's mind the thousands of small clues that, added up, point in one direction. That sack, for instance. He may have noticed, when the fowls were called for their legitimate feed of tail corn in the evening, they were slow to arrive. He might quite accidentally have looked at the

meal we had ground and noticed bits of dirt in it, or noticed the slightly floury impress of the sack where it had fallen from the granary steps. All these things he would consciously or unconsciously have tucked away into his head until enough of them made patterns, which, because they affected his business, demanded further investigation. Of course, in the sack case, more simply he may have gone into the meal-shed and counted the empty sacks to make sure the right quantity of corn had been ground, and come across the split one that way. I never asked, and I don't know!

Chapter Eight

IT WAS with Walter I had my first taste of horse-hoeing – in the humble capacity of leader: a boy's job. That is to say, I led the horse up and down the rows while Walter at the handles guided the hoe blades, cutting the weeds between the rows and close to the beet plants, leaving them on as narrow a ridge as possible so that the men who did the 'chopping out' and singling had a minimum of earth to cut with their hand hoes. We were on a bit of late-sown beet which had come up in company with a great number and variety of weeds. It was difficult to see the rows except at intervals and then only when travelling one way, when the angle of light from the sun made the smooth small beet leaves shine among the rougher and larger carlicks. The wheels of the horse-hoe were set the same distance apart as the wheels of the drill had been and in theory, if the hoes were set correctly on the toolbar, one had only to run the hoe wheels in the tracks left by the drill to be all right. But of course, when both tracks and rows were concealed by weeds, it was not so easy. We managed the first headland rows quite well: the weeds were not so vigorous there, or were more slow than the beet to push through the harder panned soil. But as we got out away from the headland it got worse and worse, and so did Walter's language.

He had acquired an unusually comprehensive

command of bad language from his time in the Army during the 1914 war. 'Tew ye!' he'd shout, and I would pull Duke's head towards me and we'd go a few yards, but not many before: 'From ye! From ye! Blast 'n sod it,' and I'd nudge Duke off to the right. So with stops and starts we crawled across the field, getting more frustrated and shorter in temper as we went. After about a couple of acres had been done and we were getting slower all the time, Walter, after a fruitless burst of 'To ye's' and 'From ye's', stopped, spat, and said: 'We ha' bin tew hun'd yards a this strike: ar sin one bloody beet an' a cut *that* bugger out.' It was hopeless. Soon after, the Guv'nor drove on to the field in his motor (they were never cars, always motors) and seeing how things stood sent us off on something else. Two days later the beet had pushed up just that fraction more, the sun caught them so they stood out boldly, and we hoed them without any more bother.

Duke wasn't a bad horse for horse-hoeing but he threw his front feet a bit wide. Bowler was the best, he would walk between eighteen inch rows and scarcely tread a plant. But none of them could touch a mare I had later in life. She was called Gypsy, was foaled on a farm near Southend, got broken winded early and was sold to a farmer in north Essex who used her for very light work only a couple of days a month. She stayed there for five years and never had a bite of oats and was out winter and summer in all weathers. I bought her cheap, and knowing her history reckoned on using her just for hoeing or perhaps light carting. She turned out to be a gem. Her wind had grown sound, she would willingly pull anything anywhere, and above all she was gentle and obedient. With her I turned horse-hoeing into a one-man job. No need for a leader – or reins either, so nicely did she move to the words of command.

At Home Farm – and it was the same over most of Suffolk – the words of command for horses were few and simple, the degree of movement required being given by changing emphasis and inflection. The command to turn to the left was 'cuppi-wi', the syllable 'wi' being drawn out and longer than the 'cuppi'. Sometimes the 'wi' would be repeated twice or more 'cuppi-wi . . . wi . . . wi' – so that the horse continued to turn, rather than just alter direction and then go straight. George told me the origin of the command was from 'come *to* me', which, since horses are always led on their near side, would mean the horse would move to the left and towards the leader. He could not tell me where 'weurdi', which means turn to the right, comes from. It is not easy in print to indicate the exact pronunciation of these words and of course they varied from man to man. One would say 'wo'rdi-i', and another something shorter like 'wodi'; 'cuppi-wi' with some sounded more like 'cubba-wia'; but the horses understood, and scarcely needed the pull on the rein to emphasize it. 'Gee up' was used for starting, but more often a click of the tongue or a familiar 'Git on then'. Sometimes you would want a horse to move forward one pace only, and for this it was 'Jis, step', and or the reverse direction 'Back abit', whereas if the horse was required to continue walking backwards the command was 'Back, back, back, hoss'.

For me it meant learning a new language almost from scratch, not only the horse commands but a vast number of words and idioms which had been current in this corner of Suffolk for centuries. 'Mawther' for instance, a Chaucerian word meaning young woman (or that's what we used it to mean), was shared by Norfolk and north Essex and is enjoying popular revival just now. Others were peculiar to Suffolk and perhaps even to the small area of the few parishes round us. There are dictionaries of the East Anglian dialects, good ones, too, which make a brave attempt to gather into their pages a comprehensive list of our words and how they are pronounced, but none is completely successful, and even now words we use daily I have not found. 'Brew' for instance, pronounced 'brue', has nothing whatever to do with brewing of any kind. This is a word for the narrow strip of land beside a ditch or a path or a hedge which, because it is too close to them, is never ploughed and becomes overgrown with grass and weeds, and, if left for too long, brambles and bushes as well. That word is in no dictionary that I know of.★ The fact of the matter is, our East Anglian tongue is not an easy one to put into print, and very few writers ever wholly succeed with it: nor can I claim to do so. The shape of sentences is quite unlike those in other dialects, our vowels are imprecise and tortured – a single E being twisted into A and back into E again; in fact if you've got two vowels in a word you've got the lot – and all in a sort of sing-song which is all right once your ear is tuned to it, but impossible for an outsider to understand. I was lucky, since a childhood in north Essex had given me an ear for something similar: I picked it up quickly.

★ Since writing this I have found 'Brew' in Forby's *Vocabulary of East Anglia*, published 1832.

Chapter Nine

FOR the first month or two I was kept at odd jobs. A day or two horse-hoeing, a day or two with Georgy, helping the pigman, carting hurdles for the shepherd, taking horses to the smithy in the next village to be shod; fetching and carrying and learning my way about. Work and sleep, work and sleep, with not a thought about entertainment, days off or relaxation. I reckon I earned my five bob a week, but the sheer pleasure of working and *belonging* to the estate was something, had I had the money, I would willingly have paid for.

For a week or more in June I did duty with the warrener, and this opened a new door on the world, because he started work as soon as it was light, a little after three in the morning, and finished near dusk, which was after ten at night-times when honest labourers were all abed. The whole estate was riddled with rabbits. There was not a bank or a ditch that hadn't its quota of holes; scarcely a tree without a burrow between the roots, and as for the old sand pits and hollows in odd corners, these were honeycombed with holes and galleries so that a ferret put down a hole in one place would bolt rabbits sixty yards away. I have an idea the warrener was not exactly on the payroll: he probably took a percentage from the sales of rabbits and pigeons he trapped and shot. Anyway, the Guv'nor seemed not to direct him very closely and he behaved in a semi-independent fashion, deciding for himself where he would trap each day unless asked to give special attention to one area – perhaps round a bit of cabbage or kale.

Vernon – the warrener – used to give me a tap on the bedroom window with a long stick just before light. I would tiptoe downstairs, through the kitchen, past the dog Rack, who slept with his head on his master's boots and growled if you went near him, and out into the morning. Rack was a half-bred, brindled collie with the most determined bad temper I've ever met in a canine. He was not allowed upstairs, but otherwise where the Guv'nor went he went also. At his heels round the fields, on the back seat of the motor – and no one ever tried twice to remove anything from the car while he was in it – or with his head on the Guv'nor's boots or, failing them, any article of clothing belonging to him. Not even Madam could shift him from guarding them. 'Come and move Rack, Father,' she'd call, 'He won't let me cross my own kitchen!' I never heard anyone, least of all his master, say a kind word to him and he repaid it with an infinite devotion and belly-crawling love. Rack had a swift, sliding, low-to-the-ground gait, which gave him the sinister appearance of perpetual readiness to spring. He would, too, biting first and barking after. If, as sometimes happened, the Guv'nor dropped his cap at the foot of the stairs, Rack would spend the night there, and on my extra early morning excursions this was a hazard. He would not suffer to be moved or allow himself to be stepped over, so I had to drop over the banisters halfway down the stairs and hope he wouldn't take offence. All in the dark and none too sure where the floor was: it added excitement and removed the cobwebs of sleep.

Vernon would be waiting for me at the corner by the horse pond. I would smell smoke and see his pipe glowing in the dark and he would whisper – for fear of waking the sleepers or starting the outdoor dog barking – that we were headed for Elm Field. This was a fifteen acre arable field in to barley, and the rabbits had already eaten the headlands bare and were working their way steadily towards the middle. We had bicycles and, without lights, rode off up the lane onto the main road, along it for half a mile, and then turned off down a sandy drift towards the wood which lay at the far end. Quite dark and silent when we left the Home yard, by the time we reached the gate into Elm Field the sky was light enough in the north-east to reflect in puddles at the drift edge, and birds which had been silent were beginning to move. As we stood at the gate I heard a thrush, or perhaps a blackbird, ruffle its feathers, and then from the depths of the still distant wood the half-cry of a cock pheasant, as if it had been disturbed before getting-up time and resented it. Dismounting, and leaving the bikes, through the gate and across the field – judging direction by the green barley rows and by bearings on a big elm against the skyline – to the most distant end of the trapline. Later on it would be dry, but our boots were soon sodden with dew and picking up earth as we walked.

Vernon had laid traps in the entrances to burrows along three sides of the field: two hundred and fifty of them, and a hundred snares in runs out on the young barley. It had been a moonless night and he reckoned we should pick up sixty rabbits or more. As we approached the wood, the occasional clink of iron

chain against stone, as rabbits struggled to free themselves from the bite of the gin, told us we had a catch.
Vernon began: he jumped down into the ditch and
quickly began to free the struggling animals from the
traps. These were laid every few yards and one in four
had a rabbit in. He opened the jaws, took the rabbits by
the back legs and head, and, with a quick pull and turn
of the wrist, killed them and threw them to me on the
field. Any traps which were empty he sprung and threw
along with the others on to the field, too. Had he
intended trapping in the same place the next night, he
would merely have covered the pressure plates of the
traps, so that no pheasant could be caught during the
day, and then come round again in the evening, to
remove the covers and sprinkle the plates with fresh
earth, which attracts rabbits. As we worked down the
length of the ditch he would call out from time to time:
'Twenty yards out you'll find a snare', or 'I set three
snares oppset the thorn bush', and I would trot out and
bring in the snare and anything it had caught.

Gin traps are horrible enough (they are illegal now):

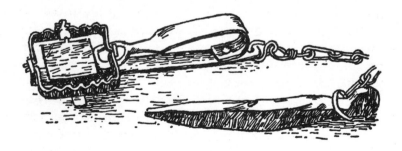

caught by one leg the rabbit struggles until the bone
breaks, and then struggles the more, turning over and

over, round and round, until the skin gives way and the poor brute is held by the tough tendons alone. Snares catch them round the neck – or well-set snares do – and often the animal is strangled pretty quickly; but sometimes as they twist and turn the wire breaks, or they pull up the peg which tethers it to the ground and go off with a tight wire round the neck to die a lingering death, down a hole, or get tangled up in a bush by the trailing wire and die there. From the hundred snares Vernon had set I took nineteen rabbits and one hare, which had somehow got caught by a front leg, but I only found eighty-odd of the snares: it was too dark to pick out the empty ones which weren't on clear runs (runs are the paths rabbits and hares make and use regularly on their way to and from the wood or burrow), and Vernon would come back later to look for them. It took about an hour to get rabbits and traps onto the headland and into the bunches of ten or a dozen that I had collected as we went along. The next thing was to 'hulk' and 'hurdle' them. Vernon was incredibly fast at this. A single quick incision in the belly with his knife, two fingers into the hole and the innards were out. Another incision between tendon and bone in a hind leg, and the foot of the other leg thrust through the slit, and the rabbit or hare was ready to hang upside down on the stout hazel sticks cut for the purpose.

He'd taken just over sixty rabbits from the traps; so in all we had seventy-nine and a hare to carry off the field to the bicycles. We did it in one journey – but I was sweating by the time we got there – and had them swinging between handlebars and another stick laid crosswise over the carrier on the back mudguard. Then

53

we had to go back for the traps and snares and add them to the load. By the time we were collected and ready to journey home to the farm it was almost a quarter to five, the sun was well up and the dew drying. We sat and smoked for a bit, wiped our bloody hands on the long wet grass under the hedge, and watched the shadows under the wood shorten and the pheasants come out and begin to scratch about on the headlands. Warreners, keepers, people who live a lot alone in woods and fields, don't talk much at any time except under the influence of beer. Their livelihood depends on accurate observations of things that move: game birds, hares and rabbits, rats, magpies, pigeons; and if you talk there is no movement: nature keeps still and watches you from hedgerow and tree and warren, instead of you watching it. Vernon said very little: a remark on the fatness of the rabbits, and on the small number of little ones we had caught, and we pushed our bikes down the drift, out on to the road and so home.

Chapter Ten

WINTER, when they are not breeding, is the best time for catching rabbits, but all the farms were so poisoned with them that the warrener was kept at it the year round. Home Farm itself had fields where on a summer evening you might count a hundred all nibbling at the same time: with field glasses, you would see three times that number on any field bordered by woods or scrub. But they were thickest at Pantons – a farm surrounded on three sides by woods and on the other by a railway cutting. The land here varied from thin flinty gravel at best to fine, almost silver sand at worst, where bracken and ling flourished and acid-indicating weeds such as spurrey, redshank and mayweed fouled the arable and pasture. Heart-breaking stuff to farm at any time, and in a dry year the returns can scarcely have paid the tithe, let alone the rent. It was in fact the kind of land we said ' 'ont keep a rabbit', yet these were just the places where they were most numerous, sleekest and fattest, and bred fastest: faster anyway than we could kill them off. I was never sure whether it was a case of land being reclaimed from heath or land returning to that condition. The fields had ill-defined boundaries, as though the plough was taken further some years than others, and there were no real hedges: just banks or lines of gorse and broom and bramble. The arable fields, spongs, many of them, were cut into by spinneys of birch and scrub, and the heathy pieces were pocked with old sandpits varying in size from a few rods to half an acre or more.

It was here, to these larger pits, Vernon and I went each day between trapping times, armed with dog, ferrets, four-ten shotguns, a bag of nets, and a narrow spade with a six-foot haft. These pits were mostly horseshoe shape, cut into the slope of the fields; the floors close-cropped weeds, the sloping walls a series of holes at every level, and between them beaten down runs, so that each one had the general appearance of an open-ended amphitheatre, the runs making the galleries, the holes so close together in places they were almost colonnaded. We approached from downwind and quietly set up a long twine net on stakes behind the pit and across the route which bolting rabbits would take for nearest wood cover. This was a three-foot net fifty yards long, and in a position which we could not cover with the guns. Then shorter nets, four feet or so in length, were set at strategic sites to left and right of the pit, Vernon choosing bends on well-trodden paths between gorse bushes, where the net was masked by greenery. Then at the foot and on the floor of the pit, in front of where we could take up our positions, he covered the most likely holes with purse-nets. This, because rabbits bolting from so close would make difficult shooting, and if shot would be so knocked about as to be unsaleable. Of the ferrets which had been scratching at their box lid. Vernon had muzzled or 'coped' one with strong linen twine before we set out; gently and quietly he picked it out and dropped it at the bottom end of the sloping wall and nipped smartly back to behind the short furze clumps where we would wait.

The ferrets had been starved overnight and this one was hungry keen. He sniffed at the first hole he came to – just one sniff – and then vanished. Two seconds later he appeared looking surprised and a little hurt. He had chased a rabbit but it had turned off somewhere underground and eluded him. Back again into the hole. Everything still: then suddenly a faint rumble underground and there, a few feet in front of me, a rabbit tightly rolled up in a purse-net. I pulled it out, untangled it and broke its neck. Vernon replaced the net: we took up our places again. A few more minutes and simultaneously we both shot, a double and a single; we left the rabbits, all three, dead where they lay. And then for half an hour it was bang bang bang. There was not time to take rabbits from the purse nets or the two side nets, but the long net at the back was safe because the dog was looking after that and he knew exactly what to do. This net had the ends curved round on itself, so that the rabbit, finding no way through, would run along until it came to the end and found itself having to turn back to get out. The dog waiting at the side lines snapped it up, rushed it round to Vernon's feet and returned for more.

After this first burst things slackened. The rabbits became more cautious, merely popping out and popping back again, giving few chances even for snap shots. Then all movement ceased. 'Reckon she've laid up', said Vernon, meaning the ferret had cornered a rabbit somewhere underground and wouldn't leave it. Being muzzled it couldn't bite or quickly kill, but would simply scratch and scratch until the rabbit died of fright and laceration. Not a pleasant end. In heavy land or on small banks where rabbit holes are shallow and short, retrieving a laid up ferret is easy. You simply fish for him with a 'line ferret'. That is, you attach a strong ten or fifteen-yard line to a collar round an unmuzzled ferret and put it down the hole where you last saw the free ferret. If it is there, the line ferret will join in and complete the massacre of the rabbit; if it is not, it will come out again and you drop him into another hole until he does find his mate. Of course sometimes the line animal will lay up against a second rabbit, but that's a chance you take. Once the line ferret is fast and you can't budge him by pulling hard on the line, all you have to do is to dig down following the line until you reach ferrets and rabbit. This is where the long handled spade is used. But in light sandy soil, and particularly in old pits, the holes are so numerous and the burrows so complex and deep that this method is unlikely to succeed. Following the path of the ferret, the line might be twenty feet down, or so turned about and back on itself that although you've twenty yards of line below ground the ferrets could be just a few feet from where it starts. Still, as Vernon explained, it's worth a trial; and for twenty minutes he 'fished' while I stood by with the gun in case any fresh rabbit should bolt. We got two or three like this and a small one which the ferret had nabbed and which was pulled out gripped tight and dead in his jaws; but he never 'laid up', and finally Vernon pulled him out and boxed him. This tactic had failed.

A coped ferret will spend perhaps an hour or more scratching away at a rabbit, but in the end he will give up. The cope is tight and uncomfortable, he is hungry and thirsty, and if he is an experienced animal he knows that only his master will relieve him. This is what the warrener banks on. He leaves the warren for a while, and on his return encourages him with rabbit guts and enticing squeaks to quit the earth. If this fails and evening comes on, he will leave a ferret box open near the earth, hoping its familiar scent will draw the beast out. On this occasion we were lucky. We were doing some short holes with the line ferret on the heathland a few hundred yards from the pit, when Vernon suddenly thrust the line into my hands and ran off to where, at the top edge of the pit, the undulating shape of the lost cope ferret was making for the woods.

How many rabbits we got that day I don't remember. The day, the pit and the bag have become blurred by so many similar excursions, each with its own tale of lines twisted round roots deep underground, of ferrets lost and ferrets found. Two of us once shot eighty-three rabbits from one pit in a morning – that's the most I remember, and it was twenty years later and on a farm in the north of the County. What I do recall is that the rabbits from the Panton Farm end were remarkably light in colour, and this is a thing I've noticed many times since; that on one part of a farm rabbits will be greyish brown and on another a sandy tan, almost yellow. Sometimes there are places where very dark grey predominates. It's a bit puzzling, since one has only to follow footprints in snow to see how rabbits will travel – and presumably mate – far from their 'home' ground. This ought to lead to a rough homogeneity, but it doesn't quite seem to. Perhaps the kind of land has something to do with it: protective colouration. The Panton rabbits were sandy tan colour on sandy soil: rabbits from the heavy clay lands in West Suffolk, I later fancied, were markedly dark, almost black-brown. It is a possible research subject which myxomatosis has since made impossible.

On our way home that night, I asked Vernon how many ferrets he had lost so far that year. He replied: 'None; none this year nor none last, neither.' I expressed surprise, if not disbelief; he turned and looked at me with a rather quizzical expression. 'If I was to lose a ferret,' he said, 'I wouldn't be a bloody fule and advertise the fact; I'd keep that to myself and say nothen. Then when the old women in the village come squarking how their hins hev bin killed, that 'ont be nothen ter do with me!' This was a piece of information I should have treasured more closely. Ten years later, when I let slip I'd lost a ferret near the village, three people placed the death of tame rabbits at my door and two more of hens which were found dead and drained; and there was no way out of this with honour except by paying up! Since then I've been more careful. There are also dreadful stories of ferrets crawling into prams . . . which I don't believe.

I learned a lesson of a different kind from another warrener who used to come in from time to time on Saturday afternoons, when, farmwork being done, I was free to do what I liked. And I liked rabbiting – maybe because being young and quick I could hold my own with the gun. Even experienced shots are hard put to it to equal the speed and accuracy of a well-trained lad at bolting rabbits. It happened that one afternoon the warrener put a ferret into an earth, and when a few moments later a rabbit appeared at the mouth of another hole I shot and killed it. No more bunnies appeared, and in due course the man walked over, picked up the dead rabbit – and, to my horror, a dead ferret, too. I apologized; said how sorry I was; explained what was obvious – that I didn't see the ferret because the rabbit was in front of it. But clearly, apologies were not enough. This he claimed was his best ferret; a fine worker; an animal he prized above all others and due shortly to produce a large and valuable litter of baby ferrets. Thus he had lost two sources of income at one blow. My suggestion that ten bob would cover the damage was met with silence; a quid, with a reiteration of the virtues of the departed. He finally settled for twenty-five bob – my wages for five weeks – and I went home to tell the sad tale to Georgy, who was feeding the pigs. The other chaps would have hooted. Georgy was too kind and too good a friend to laugh; he simply put the facts of the case and let me see for myself how I had been done. The best ferret in the whole of old England was worth seven and six at the outside. Any the warrener might have would be worth around three bob. As for that particular one being near kindling – would he use a heavily pregnant ferret? Was it indeed a doe at all? Having been asked this question I recollected the chap referring to the beast as 'old man' as he took it out of the box – so I had been done again. Naturally I was indignant: I thought the fellow a rogue. He had taken advantage of my ignorance and innocence and traded on my good will. That was my view at the time, and no one would say it was not justified. But since then, looking back with a cooler eye, I can see the warrener's point of view with more detachment and sympathy. I never paid him.

Chapter Eleven

ALTHOUGH the entire Home Farm household went to bed with the hens in summer time and between seven and eight in the winter, the Guv'nor didn't stay there all night. It was his habit – unbroken for twenty years – to get up at one or two in the morning, dress, and go round the stables and the yards to see that all was well. I was sometimes woken by the creak of the barn door or the sudden stirring of bullocks in the yard as he went his rounds, and occasionally voices came in at the bedroom window and, looking out, I would see his shadowy figure talking to another, which might be the village policeman or a keeper. The policeman was an elderly, good-natured man whose ambition was to live a quiet life. There was no major crime, anyway, and he was active in pursuing minor offenders – poachers mainly – only so far as was necessary to keep on good terms with the shooting gentry and local magistrates. I never saw him on the farm during daylight hours and I never heard anything ill of him from the men. He did once stop me on the road, though.

I was driving a lorry-load of sugar beet pulp from the factory to the farm when he walked out of his front gate and held up his hand. The lorry was an alleged fifty horsepower ex-army Pierce-Arrow: a great high machine on solid tyres, with a four-foot gear lever and pedals so heavy to operate that I had to use both feet at

once on the brake or clutch, and bracing myself against the steering wheel at the same time push down before they would budge. I had been carting pulp for several days, and on most of them had seen and waved to the policeman. I pulled up, and he walked over looking very official. 'Just let me hev a look at your driving licence, my boy,' he said. I told him it was at home. 'Oh, you orter carry that with you, you know – you'd better bring that along and show me termorra; and, while you're on it, do you tell your Guv'nor that that'd be best if he get a road fund licence for your lorry and insurance too,' and with that he waved me on. When I told the Guv'nor, all he said was we would have to send the other lorry to the factory in future, and use this one for carting on roads away from the town . . . which, though he did not say so, would be off our policeman's beat.

In the end, though, the lorry was licensed. The Guv'nor carried off a big deal with a feeding stuffs factory where there had been a serious fire. He bought the entire stock as it stood for a few shillings a ton. Some was burnt, much spoiled by water from the fire-hoses; but there were still many tons of perfectly sound feed. For two weeks both lorries were going backwards and forwards, getting first the most perishable stuff – the partly-wet and partly-burned feed – and later the good stuff. Our livestock had never lived so well – or I suspect so dangerously, because there were tons of bags without description, and it was a matter of guesswork whether they should be fed in bulk or merely sprinkled in the feed. There was white and green fish meal, poultry spice, barleymeal, middlings, flaked maize, linseed, cotton and groundnut cake, castor oilseed cake, bran, milo, alfalfa meal and milk powder. Bags of oystershell, flint grit, bags of derris powder for warble dressing, 'bluestone' for dressing wheat seed, and bags of seeds which no one could recognize at all. It was all stacked in heaps in the barn and granary – the stuff we knew in one area and the doubtful piles in another, and the whole staff was called in to sniff and test on the tips of their tongues what this or that might be.

Georgy and I really enjoyed mixing the pig grub after that. A nice thick layer of creamy-coloured middlings, a thin one of bran, a bit more of bean meal, a layer of green alfalfa meal, a dusting of red poultry spice ('that 'ont hurt 'em, and do we don't use it up the wet'll soak through and rot it!'), and a top coat of milk powder. It smelt marvellous and when we put in our shovels and cut down through the heap, the strata were exposed; layers of incomparable goodness. The Guv'nor bought in extra pigs to eat up the damp stuff before it heated and got mouldy, and we were kept busy mixing and feeding and mixing again long past normal times. Every animal on the place came in for food bonuses, and everything looked the better for it. In particular, the horses: George added a handful or two of linseed cake at each bait and their coats shone with it. In fact, George's pair went on having that extra bloom for months after the others' horses had reverted to the normal well-groomed look – but this was because George (as he admitted privately to me) – 'kep a few bags for the rainy days.' He knew all too well that linseed and the like would not again find its way into the mangers except by happy accident. The Guv'nor was not over-generous with horsefeed. He couldn't afford to be.

'We are going to church tomorrow morning; you'd better clean your shoes tonight.' I had been waiting with some apprehension for this announcement. Madam and the Guv'nor knew I was a Quaker, but had made it a condition of pupillage that when the family went to church I should go too. I had no wish to go – certainly felt no need – but, severed from my Quaker background and totally immersed in this new life, if church-going was routine then I was content. More than that, I wanted to conform. I happily accepted the almost ritualistic nature of the farm work for six days and welcomed the chance of taking part in the rich and solemn rituals of a Church of England service on the seventh. The apprehension arose from my lack of knowledge of the service. Some slight familiarity with

65

the Prayer Book and Bible did not help, and I was anxious lest ignorance should lead me into doing the wrong thing and bring disgrace on me and the family. Still, in the spirit of conformity and optimism, and with clean shoes, I joined the family in a walk across the fields, through the iron side-gate and into church. The Guv'nor didn't come: he had, as he said, 'things to attend to' – a statement heard without surprise, since he put his foot in the church door at Harvest Festival and funerals only.

We took our seats and waited for the parson. I looked round, read the hymn board and the ten commandments, and tried to read the memorials on the walls and the faces of the congregation without losing any reverence of expression. A man the other side of the aisle smiled at me. Who the . . . was he? Something about the face was familiar – the nose or the moustache – someone I knew a long time ago? I had almost given up, baffled, when he put up his hand to brush a fly from his face and exposed his waistcoat and watch-chain. This I knew at once. It was George: completely disguised by a bare head. I had never before seen him without a cap, and never did for thirty years more, until he was ill and I went to see him at home and in bed. George would tilt his cap forward to keep the sun out of his eyes and tip it backwards to mop the sweat on his brow – but, out of doors anyway, that was the limit. It never came right off.

The bell stopped tolling and we waited. The congregation seemed a little restless; hob-nailed boots scraped on the stone floor, men coughed and women shushed their children. I didn't know what we were waiting for, but obviously, whatever it was, it ought to

66

have happened by now. The organist got up from her seat and went to the door. Heads turned to watch her; she went out into the porch and then turned back, pausing on her way to the organ to tell Madam, 'He's now a'coming.' It was the parson − later than usual, so I gathered. The congregation rose as the little white-haired man walked down the aisle. He was smiling; he waved his hands in half-made, friendly, benevolent gestures, halting now and then to look round at his parishioners. They seemed to be avoiding his eye. There was a feeling of suspense; of waiting for something dramatic to happen − or was it a feeling of embarrassment?

The parson reached the chancel, and then turned very quickly and, almost trotting, went through the curtained doorway of the vestry. The congregation sighed. Men looked at their wives; wives shushed the children again and we all shuffled some more. We waited. My nose tickled. The wooden pew was hard. I tried to work out the date of the nearest memorial − *hic jacet* somebody *MDCCVI*. The organist hopped down from her perch and spoke to a man near the pulpit. I couldn't hear what they were saying, but he got up and disappeared through the vestry curtain. Could the parson be drinking communion wine, I wondered? The man came out, nodded to the organist and sat down. The curtain twitched, parted, and the parson appeared. At least he half appeared, retreated and then came out with (confirming my suspicions) a bottle. But it wasn't − it was a galosh. Black, muddy round the edges, he held it low in front of him as he walked towards the chancel, bent down and carefully placed it at the foot of the brass lectern. This, I began to feel sure, was not to be an ordinary service.

The old man stood for a few moments looking down at the shoe; turned and looked towards the altar and the tall East window; turned again to face us, and in a remarkably strong clear voice began 'Our Father', which the congregation took up under the confident leadership of the organist. But we had scarcely reached 'Thy Will be Done' when the parson seemed to lose interest: he looked round for the galosh, picked it up and suddenly announced 'Hymn number . . .'; but before we could reach for our hymn books or the organist could strike a note – for this was not one of the numbers on the board – he called us to prayer. The congregation, or that part which was not still standing and prepared to sing, got down on their knees. 'Now let they servant depart in Peace.' The words were spoken in conversational tone and were apparently a prelude to the sermon, for he went up the pulpit steps, came down again to retrieve the galosh, mounted the steps once more and began: 'The flood was a frightful thing . . . Noah and Jonah were afraid, there were whales, and the cricket ground, although it is owned by the church, is part of the larger mission field where Jacob laboured for seven years, nor, in witnessing this marriage. . . .'

He went on and on, mixing Biblical phrases with items of parish news, stopping now and then to wave his arms or silently fix the congregation in a long stare before picking up again the tangled threads of his disordered address. He spoke cultivated sounding nonsense. I was embarrassed and sad for him and was infinitely relieved when the organist, taking matters into her own hands, began to play *The Old Hundredth*. So we stood and sang and drowned the parson's sermon. He seemed not to mind and sung a verse himself, before, clutching his galosh, he made off down the aisle, through the door and out into the graveyard. We followed after. And for once in my life I had the tact to say nothing. Nor was anything of the matter said to me, except that Madam remarked the parson had been ill for a while and was, alas, no better.

I was not further required to honour the religious observances part of my contract. You may think this parson out of the ordinary; and perhaps, inasmuch as he remained in office there for several years carrying on in the same way, he was extraordinary. Yet half of the ten or so parishes where I have lived have been served by priests whom the less reverent villagers would describe as 'daft', or 'a bit soft', or 'not quite right in the head, poor chap!' The dividing line between eccentricity and madness is a narrow one, but most of these came out firmly on the far side. At my next farm, for instance, the parson was not regarded as mad, but odd. I thought so, too, when I asked him to shut our yard gate as he passed through, he spat straight in my face. Not long after I did duty, along with my boss, in restraining him from violent action against his housekeeper, and learned from his ravings something of the horrors arising from a repressed life. This man was finally taken away and (I believe) certified; but whether that was actually the case I don't know, for after a year or so he returned to take up his work in the village and became widely known for his preaching. It was strange to see people from distant villages arriving – even by car – to hear, as they told me, eloquent sermons, the product of a great intellect tempered by a warm humanity. Poor fellow, a few years and the disease overtook him once more, so he was 'put away' and died without ever preaching again.

Chapter Twelve

UNTIL the Great War, for five or six generations, the village had been dominated by the family which owned it and the two or three thousand acres around. This was no longer the case, but memorials in the church and headstones in the graveyard showed they had a good tenure and had contributed their quota of young men for glorious sacrifice in distant parts of the Queen's Empire, and for service in the church itself; cornets and curates, captains and canons. Perhaps too much of their bright young blood had been spilled on desert sand; perhaps the too steady-seeming revenue from the estate had sapped their enterprise. I was told that for two generations none of them had made a 'good' marriage. And by 'good' one understands an alliance which brings money with it − without which few landowning families ever survive.

By the nineteen twenties the family had sold the village and the farms, retaining only the park and the house (which was called The Park) and a couple of grass fields by the church. The old Squire lived alone at The Park with a housekeeper, two maids and a man who acted as gardener, groom, keeper, and back'us boy. Not that there was a lot of gardening to do − one flower bed under the drawing-room window and a patch in the walled kitchen garden where old hens and cabbages and weeds fought it out, while rabbits kept the lawns short. Nor was there much grooming: a pair of riding horses and a riding pony which grazed on the park and never saw saddle from one year's end to the next. Gamekeeping was confined to an occasional night prowl with the constable round the bits of woodland on the park and to supplying the Squire with young rabbits during the week or, in season, game birds for Sundays.

Yet although the Squire was apparently cut off from the village, had no power over people's lives and could not – as his forebears had done – build up or break men by exercise of favour or disfavour, support or evict, cherish or destroy – although his power was gone, his authority remained. He was still 'Squire' in a way the new owner of his lands never succeeded in becoming, and his views were taken into account in the village. He himself never went beyond the park gates, but word came down from him to his groom, from groom to housekeeper, and it was she who saw to it that the old man's wishes were known beyond the gates. Her message was passed to an ex-servant, who in turn spread the news to the post office; and from there – as with most rural post offices – the news travelled faster than the Royal Mail. How the Squire on his side found out what was going on in the village I never discovered, but he did, and none of the children of his former employees got married but a small money present came from his hand – down through the usual line of communication. I never clapped eyes on him, and only once went into the park or the two grass fields by the church which were rented by the Guv'nor. But the Guv'nor saw him twice a year – Lady Day and Michaelmas – presumably to pay the hire. Georgy said the only time he ever had to clean his motor was for these two events — and funerals.

The real Squire — if that is how he must be described — was of very different mettle: a successful second-generation merchant, whose business extended far beyond the county boundaries and seemed to thrive equally in good times and bad. I did see him several times. He used to ride down the lane and through the yard on a well-polished hack once every month. He sat upright, well-groomed like his horse but with a much less kind expression in his eye. Perhaps my feelings about him were coloured by the Guv'nor's: he couldn't stand him — and obviously the feeling was reciprocated in full. Whenever that rider came in sight the Guv'nor quickly retired to the house; even the men moved out of vision if they could — there was something cold and malevolent in his eye, some suppressed fury, only visible in the constant chewing of his moustache, which totally unnerved us all. If a meeting was unavoidable, he would either not look at all — perhaps even looking in the opposite direction; or he would look, but only acknowledge the time of day with a curt nod, combined with — and this was truly horrifying — a drawing back of his lips from his teeth, so that he appeared to be on the point of snapping. The chaps always said: 'He never smiles — he only show his teeth' and the Guv'nor said, if he ever saw him smile, he expected the rent to go up. The trouble was, he was not just a hard man, for that is a quality we could understand and perhaps even admire. Fair's fair, and a bargain's a bargain, and rent is rent. But he was mean with it and this put him beyond the pale. In some respects he may have been a better landlord than the old squire — almost certainly less capricious – I wouldn't know; but he would have had to be *a great deal* better to have overcome this major disability. He seemed incapable of a kind word or a generous gesture – and without these he was not . . . well . . . he was not a *gentleman.* Poor fellow; he succeeded in making money and enemies enough for a dozen; lived unloved and died unlamented. Later, of course, I came to wonder what frightful event had twisted and warped him, what bitter nurse or sorry schooling had divorced him from humanity; but at the time, whenever he rode through the yard, we all smelt sulphur and drew back into the shadows until he had passed.

Mark you, I half suspect that, cut off though he was, the 'old Squire' was not above a little malicious needling of the new man. There was one time when the village was about to celebrate a national event – I don't remember whether it was a Royal wedding or a Jubilee or what – but before the parish council could get round to asking the new Squire, the old Squire sent (via the housekeeper to the chairman) a cheque for sixty pounds towards the jollity. This, if he ever knew about it, must have been a poser for the new man. First, the celebrations were being held in the park, where he would not be welcome; and second, if he contributed anything, it would either have to equal the old Squire's donation, or, to reinforce his position, it would have to exceed it. Nothing, you might think, would be simpler than to take one of these courses. But (as I read it) the old Squire had played the ace of trumps. The population of the village numbered under two hundred, and sixty pounds was already far more money than was needed to ensure the wild success of any fête. In fact, it

73

was too much. Had the new man given more than sixty pounds, he would have exposed himself as a buyer of popularity: had he given less, he would have accepted the seal of secondary status in the community. In the event he chose wisely, and, hoping to avoid scorn on either count, gave nothing. But, of course, we held it against him none the less. 'All that money he've got, and he 'ould'nt give nothen f' the jamboree – stingy ol' bugger !'

The fête turned out to be a huge success. The organizing committee, consisting entirely of men, voted for spending all the money on the one day and most of it on beer. The difficulty was that allowing a gallon a head for the men of the parish and half a gallon for the boys it only added up to under a hundred gallons – and in money terms this meant only eleven pounds or so, which was thought to be a ridiculously small proportion of the amount available. What head-scratching and heart-searching went on in the committee will never be known, but in the end it was decided that, instead of mild beer – which was what we always drank – it was to be old ale. This set the balance moving in the right direction, but with leeway still to make. So, in the end, on top of a hundred gallons of *old* ale, five dozen bottles of light and dark (for the ladies), two bottles each of sherry and port, six of whisky, six of gin, and crates of lemonade and ginger beer, there was money left for enough beef and ham to feed everyone twice over and for prizes for the sports which were to be held in the afternoon. The beer was housed in a small ante-room of the parish hall, and for some unexplained reason I was put in charge of it. I remember the early part of the day – the chaps who

74

were moving tables and chairs got hot and thirsty and needed refreshment. I remember the lunch rush when the beer wouldn't flow fast enough from the spigot. I remember the cool dark bite of that old ale – the first pint, the second, the third, perhaps even the fourth. After that I was (so I am told) assisted to a seat on the floor at the back of the hall, and joined the village's one teetotaller – a Salvationist who had been pressed to a nice pint of lemonade (three-quarters clear London Gin) – in singing, and later, alas, in feeling very ill indeed.

God bless the Squire and all his relations! There was scarcely a man could stand upright unaided by five o'clock, and anyone who was moving by ten o'clock – as Georgy said, 'You could hear th' old beer a'swoshing about in them.' It's maybe more pleasant to recollect that, although virtually the whole parish was awash with strong ale for thirty-six hours, the only damage done was to a chair and – or so stable gossip had it – one young woman. As both were of an age when treatment such as they received would inevitably be followed by alteration to their shapes, this was not in any way thought to be an excessive price to pay for such a jamboree. Besides, the local wheelwright mended the chair, and in due time a wedding ceremony made the girl respectable too.

The thing was, of course, that jollifications such as this fête were for the village and the village only. Few people strayed in from outside unless they happened to be young men courting our girls or visiting their relatives. Few beyond walking distance could come even if they wanted to. There was no handy bus service: no farm-worker had a car; none I knew of had a motorcycle, and indeed at Home Farm only the threshing men and one or two others had even push bikes. If we went anywhere, we walked. A few miles to the west of us, the railway; nearer — less than three miles — a main London-to-seaside motor road, packed at week-ends with cars and coaches; but, although geographically so close to these arteries and well served with roads to reach them, for some reason the village was isolated from it all. Cars went past the road to the village street; they never stopped. And I think, since customs and language lingered here long after they had vanished from more remote-seeming places, it must have been this way for centuries: a small backwater, a place to one side of anywhere.

All this made for a closed community: everyone knew everyone else and his business. There is no hiding of weakness under these circumstances, which is perhaps why it was an honest place. You could leave your jacket, with a wallet in the pocket, hanging on a post all day and never imagine it would be interfered with. And of course, if it was, you would probably get to know within minutes who did it. The country is all eyes and ears. You are alone, walking through a wood maybe or down a narrow footpath between high hedges: you can't be seen. But the chap hoeing three fields away will hear the panicky treble clap of the pigeon clattering out of an ivied tree or the alarm call of a blackbird, see a rook or jackdaw pull up in passage and circle twice, high above where you are moving. Automatically he will mark your invisible progress, until he is satisfied who you are and what you are up to. It is one of the saddest things about the modern countryman that he no longer uses his eyes and ears, or indeed any other of his senses, in this way; he is relatively oblivious to what is going on around him and unaware of what he is missing. And, alas, this oblivion extends to his work, too. The tractor driver goes on, regardless of what he may be doing to the land, where the oldster behind his team not only saw and heard what his implement was doing but felt through the soles of his boots what was happening inches below the harrow teeth or drill coulter.

Chapter Thirteen

QUITE unexpectedly one morning the Guv'nor put me on to drilling with Willy. This was the first job of any responsibility with the horsemen I had been given. And it wasn't all that responsible either, because the Spring corn and the roots, which had to be drilled with great accuracy, were already in and up, and this was but the fag-end of drilling – rye-grass and clover under barley. The barley was three inches high, and we were to cross-sow with a mixture of red clover and rye-grass which would be left, after the barley was harvested, for hay (or more properly 'stover') the following year. With the barley to some extent masking the smaller seeds it was unlikely, even if I allowed the drill to block for a few yards, that it would be discovered. I was glad of this, because there was a system and scale of penalties for this crime. A single blocked coulter right across the field cost twopence. A whole drill-width missed meant a fine of a shilling; and on five bob a week I could not afford many of those.

It was on this morning I learned a new lesson. The team for the job consisted of George the head horseman and his pair, and Willy with his. Full of enthusiasm, and seeing that both Willy and George were harnessed up and ready to leave the stable, I got hold of Willy's second horse and led it from the stable and across to the lane. I heard George say something to

78

Willy as I clattered out and took no thought of it, but when he joined me in the lane I saw by his face that I had done something very wrong indeed. He was dark red with rage. 'Who do you think you are a–hustling out afront of me?' he said. I just hadn't understood. Our comings and goings were better ordered than I knew. It was the head horseman's privilege to leave the stable first, *and* – George pointed this out to me as well, lest I should fall into error later on – his privilege to go into the field first. I said I was sorry and explained that I didn't know, but it took several days before we were on kindly terms again. To me the row seemed out of proportion, but then I didn't know and could not have understood just what it meant to be head horseman. It was not an idle title nor won lightly, and respect should be paid to whom it is due. As it turned out – and perhaps George associated what happened that day with the way it began – the day was a disaster.

Turning from the lane across the ditch into the field, the near-side wheel of George's tumbril somehow dislodged part of the ditch bank, sunk under the weight of load and slowly tipped over on to its side. There was a horrible splintering crack as the horse, struggling to keep upright against the pressure, broke the shafts – stout four-by-four ash though they were – and George, who had been thrown clear as the cart tipped, ran to his head. Willy quickly tied his horse short to the gate-post and bade me tie mine with the flat-roll to the drill, and then we went to help. The danger with an overturned cart is mainly that the frightened horse, in an endeavour to be free, will do itself an injury. And where the shafts are broken or splintered, as they were now, if the beast struggled there was a good chance that a long wooden

79

splinter or even some part of the cart-irons would make a serious wound. Unfortunately George – instead of one of his usual quiet well-trained pair – had a young horse in the shafts, and his first concern was to hold it still and prevent it from further panic. He was a small man, and the frightened horse – still held by the weight of the cart from moving forwards – was trying all the time to buck and rear.

'Put your coat over his hid, time I can hold on!' he shouted. 'Steady, hoss, blast you, steady now . . . damn it, hurry up with that coat – do he'll have my arms off!' The coat, acting as a blindfold, did have a quieting effect and the horse stood trembling. 'He ain't hu't hisself yet,' said Willy. 'No, but he damn soon will if we don't git him outen this – there's a bloody gret sharp splinter a-pressing on his ribs, and if he go forrard hard that'll drive into him.' That spike was the danger. Then Willy had an idea: he got his dinner bag – an old army haversack – and cutting the wide webbing strap from it bound this about the shaft so as to cover the splinter, but with one turn of webbing within the splint, so that, if the bandage slipped as the horse moved and the point did dig into its flesh, the webbing would tighten and the point would break off short and not cause a deep wound. Then we set about unharnessing the horse as it stood. First the back-strap and britchen chains; next the top-latch, so that the animal was unattached at both ends; and last the belly girth, so the pad would slip off as it moved. All this time, of course, the horse was being gripped and nipped by the angle of the shafts. It was not easy, and it had to be done quietly and quickly: any sudden jump by the horse and we'd have been in a proper mess.

When all was free, and with Willy and me pulling the shafts apart with all our strength, George firmly and slowly allowed the horse to edge forwards. This he accomplished for half a step, but then it became uncontrollable, and with a great heave it burst out and into the field with George hanging on as best he could. It was all right. There was a wound, a four-inch gash across the ribs on one side, and a patch of raw skin on the other, and that was all. I thought we would go back home and tend the wounded horse, but George said no. It wasn't bad enough. The wounds would be clear of any harness when he was in chains (meaning the 'plough chains' used for drawing the harrows), and anyway the seed ought to go in that day. So we went to work. George went ahead with his harrows across the field and we followed with the drill; Willy steering, and me walking behind putting off and on the seed at the headland turns and watching the drill tubes and coulters didn't block. By bait time, George with his wide gang of light harrows had almost finished ahead of us. When he did, he unhitched the harrows, tied his young horse to the overturned cart – was there a psychological reason for this choice when a good gatepost was handy? – put the other horse in the flat roll and rolled away after us. He finished only a few minutes after we did, and leaving cart and harrows in the field we went home.

Back in the stable, baiting the horses, Willy remarked: 'Tha's a funny thing th' ole man never come along time we was a' drillen.' 'Ahh . . . but he did,' said George. 'I see him drive past in his motor. He slow down when he see the cart in the ditch; he didn't stop, but I'll bet he know what the damage is b' now, and I doubt we'll hear about it afore turning-out time.' I was rather expecting ructions when I went into supper that evening but the Guv'nor just asked who had been driving the horse when it happened and whether the horse was hurt, and that was that. He knew the gateway, the horse and George, and what was reasonably avoidable and what was not. The matter was not mentioned again. It is worth recording that the seeds we drilled that day germinated just as drought set in, never came to anything and were ploughed in with the barley stubble – a thing which happened more often in those days than now. While writing this, it occurs to me it was odd George should have used a flat roll that day. The rib or Cambridge roll was more customary; perhaps it was being used elsewhere.

Pigeons plagued the estate crops. In spring and early summer they went mad on green peas and early cabbage; in high summer they went for the peas which would be harvested dry – Harrison's Glory; and in winter for the kale and cabbages, turnips, and clovers. In our thickly wooded parish there was cover enough for tens of thousands, and they made good use of it. From May until September their cooing was almost the dominant sound, and they nested in the holly bushes and ivy and the tall hedgerows for a month or more longer than that. Practically the only time of the year when they were not damaging crops was when the acorns had fallen: for two or three weeks they would be stuffing themselves with unbelievable numbers of them. What the record take of acorns from a pigeon's crop is I don't know, but twenty or more was common – and not small acorns either. They were so tightly packed in their crops and so heavy that often the birds could only just flutter from the ground to their perches overhead, where they would sit stuffed and waiting on digestion. If farmwork was slack, and the pigeons making a particularly concerted attack on a crop, the Guv'nor would fill my pockets with cartridges, hand me the farm gun – an ancient twelve-bore with damascus barrels so worn and thin 'you could cut wads with them', as the saying goes – and off I'd trot – glad to be going, since, after muck-carting or whatever it was, this was by way of being a holiday.

I remember one morning being sent to a field of peas which, just as they were on ready to pick, the pigeons had discovered and were busy ruining them. The warrener was to go to the far end of the field, some four hundred yards away; and I was to tuck down in the ditch, well screened by brambles and tall sheep's parsley between two lofty elms; an ideal spot. We set out together, and were in position before four o'clock with our 'coy' birds set out among the peas well within gunshot. These decoys were dead pigeons which the warrener had shot the day before. They were carefully chosen: their feathers had to be undamaged, lest the birds they were intended to decoy down should be suspicious. They were set head to wind, with their heads held up by means of a sharpened stick, thinner than a pencil, upright in the ground and up through the base of the head. To make them more lifelike, their eyelids were cut off, so the eyes were open and shining.

Pigeons are normally acutely nervous, and quick to notice anything out of the ordinary. Stick a coy out in the field the wrong way for the wind and you can wait all day – none of its fellows will come to it. But sometimes – it can be because they are ravenously hungry –

83

they will go mad and, almost ignoring danger signals, float down to feed even among dead and wounded birds. In times of plenty, I think, this only happens with young peas, and when there is only one field for some miles. On this morning they did act mad. I had hardly squatted in the ditch when a pair settled beside my coys and began feeding. Beginner's luck. Both fell to one barrel, and I scrambled out to turn them into coys, too; set them up – and before I could get under cover more birds came down to join them, and I shot another. This I left

where it fell; there was no need to move it, for the pigeons were taking no care; they just lusted after peas, and although they flew up with each shot it was only moments before they were back again. What was happening – and it was planned to happen – was that when the warrener fired, the birds he scared fled to my end of the field, and when I fired they made the return journey, and at each turn lost one or two of their number to our guns. By a quarter to seven my cartridges were gone, and stringing up fifty-seven dead pigeons I went home to breakfast, leaving the warrener, who had come better supplied, to carry on. He shot until ten and brought back over a hundred. Later in the afternoon we went again to the field – this time choosing different hides – and shot another forty between us. This seemed to do the trick, because on the following day only odd birds were feeding there, and the day after that scores of women and children pickers came in and the crop was soon in bags and away.

Incidentally it was those same bags which led to an unhappy incident. Bags, whether for potatoes or peas or greens, were always a nuisance. The London wholesalers just bundled them up in hundreds and sent

them to the farms in any sort of condition. Some with small holes, some with the bottoms out, and some so rotten that when filled and dropped they burst, and the pickers wasted time scooping the contents into a fresh bag. To avoid this, the Guv'nor sent Tom, Albert, Olly and me to sort over a thousand which the London lorry had dumped in the barn at Pantons.

The day was warm, the barn was dim, and after we had been sorting for a bit we began to sweat and then to itch. Tom stopped to scratch his leg; Olly (he and Albert were regular casual workers on the estate) remarked, 'Suthen was wholly tittlen him round his belly band,' and Albert undid the straps of his 'lijahs' the better to rub at the irritation. I reckoned the bags had itching powder in them and opened the big double door to let light in and dust out, scratching as I did so. As darkness gave way to light, the three men bent down to look more closely at the bags and then sprang back. 'Blast it, them bags is lousy!' cried Tom. And so they were. Fleas in their thousands, so thick they might be counted in pints, were like a living carpet all over bags and floor. Small sharp-set fleas accustomed to the rich pastures of the East End and starved during their long journey into Suffolk were seeking a quick meal from honest countrymen. 'They're all over me, I got more fleas than a sick cat,' said Albert. 'I'm being etten alive – the little sods is crawling round me ear'oles,' wailed Olly. Tom took off his jacket and started shaking it about to dislodge them. Of course this was no good; the little brutes were on our legs, arms, bodies and heads: we were infested. And how they bit, bit, crawled, hopped and bit again; it was not to be borne.

Since at that time middle-aged countrymen never

exposed more of their persons to daylight – or for that matter lamplight either – what happened next is a measure of how hard-pressed we were, how viciously we were being attacked. Each occupying a distant corner of the barn and turning our backs to each other, we stripped. Unheard-of public activity! Struggling out of jackets and waistcoats, leather-strapped trousers, long underwear, we flapped and scratched, shook our clothes, beat our breasts, rubbed and slapped and swore all at the same time. 'Wish'd I had a bit of soap,' said Olly. 'Yes,' said Tom, 'I could do with a bar of wet Monkey Brand; there's millions on 'em, they're flat and won't crack!' I looked over my shoulder. It was a scene this ancient barn had never seen equalled. Four pale, white, almost luminous bodies, hopping and slapping, brushing and twitching, scratching and jabbering with vexation. A corybantic frenzy. It was at this moment we heard a motor stop outside. Panic! A frantic untangling of long-legged pants and long-sleeved vests, a mad search in the half-light for trousers, but before anyone could get decent, in walks the Guv'nor. This was the only time I ever knew him at a loss for words: he simply couldn't believe his eyes. His men, in his barn, *naked* . . .! 'What . . . what . . . what the devil are you doing together . . .? What *are* you up to . . . going swimming perhaps, eh?' He looked at me as though suspicious I might be the instigator of this extraordinary exhibition. But before I could begin to explain, he bent down and with one horny finger began to scratch at his ankle, and Tom burst out, 'Tha's right, Master, do you stand there by them bags fra minute and you'll hatter her yourn off too – they're alive wi' fleas and the little sods hev driv us dam' near crazy!'

87

The Guv'nor began to see and feel the point. 'Well, don't just stand there, get you dressed together and then pitch the bags into the pond and drown them. You can pull them out this afternoon.' And not waiting to play host to more of those East Enders, off he went.

We did as we were bid and 'drowned' the bags, but at supper time I was still suffering minor attacks which had me restless and added to everyone's amusement as the Guv'nor told the tale. But I had a bit of a laugh myself, since I noticed the large bar of soap was missing from its usual place in the dairy and the Guv'nor was wearing an uncommonly smart suit for a week-day evening.

To go back to pigeons, our rate of killing was nothing exceptional; real professors of the art will shoot five or six hundred a day, under less ideal conditions than we had. Since it was something I did pretty well (the chaps said 'he wholly hold it straight!'), I enjoyed pigeon shooting. Not only for the actual shooting, but as much for where it was done. Secret places; small bowers in thick hedges; deep, mossy-banked ditches overhung with ash, maple, thorn and nuttry; alcoves in the thick ivy of a great elm. Spending hours on end in these I got to know them as a young man knows his girl – with all the senses. The scent of bruised wild mint or of young thorn leaves in spring; the pungent dusty odour of ivy; the penetrating, sweetly-acrid scent peculiar to chestnut leaves in autumn. Each of these, and hundreds more, made their first and most powerful impression on me whilst after pigeons.

I would sit with my gun across my knees, alert to every movement – peering through the screen of leaves or twigs at the sky, waiting for a sight of the sickle-shaped wings and for the peculiar changes in wing-beat, which signify either that the bird is coming closer for a look at my coy, or is sheering off with a sudden twist (which will be noted by others) because it does not like what it sees. Sometimes, when things were slow, I would become absorbed watching insects climb the grasses round my feet, or the hedge birds. A robin once spent a whole day within a few feet of me and even perched on my gun barrel, with head cocked, curious, seemingly careless of the dead pigeons on the bank beside me. I was absorbed in the small world of a few feet of ditch – day-dreaming, I don't doubt – but at that age reacting in split seconds to the phee phee phee of pigeon wings and ready with measuring eye to bring it down in a heap of bloody feathers.

It never crossed my mind – nor anyone else's in those days – that perhaps the best way of ensuring a large native population of pigeons is to shoot them in winter. This sounds contradictory, but there is some basis for thinking it is so. Most pigeons die during winter of cold and starvation. If they are left unmolested in a bad winter, particularly a snowy one, they rapidly eat all the clovers down to the ground. This is their main diet, and when the clover is done they starve. The more pigeons there are, the quicker this will happen – and few will survive to breed next season. But if a lot of pigeons are shot, then the limited food supplies will last longer – long enough to ensure that most, if not all, will survive the winter and breed again.

At most, we kept a few thousand pigeons off our crops some of the time. In summer they were mostly wood pigeons, which we called 'dows', but later (and we believed from Norway), came endless flocks of blue rocks – smaller, darker birds, but with the same appetites for our crops. We never ate pigeons, and the heaps we shot went to the local market and were sold for a few pence each. Even the men, who at that time were short of meat, were not keen on them. There was a superstition that if you ate any number you would become incorrigibly bound, and I heard dreadful tales of men who had eaten one every day for a week and died of bowels set fast. They may indeed be slightly constipating, and perhaps for the countryman, whose morning duties were performed in a draughty two-seater at the bottom of the garden, constipation and a long wait in the cold were not welcome.

The best man for pigeons in the parish was the estate keeper. He set decoys so naturally that I once fired both barrels into his flock and was horrified when he rose up from his hide, asking what the bloody hell I thought I was a-doing of? I felt foolish, and went away to the far end of the field to set my wooden coy bird up – I had borrowed one from the warrener – and it was here that I saw something I think must be unique. No sooner was I under cover than a pigeon came swooping down and, alighting beside the coy, jumped on its back and attempted to mate with it. I was so astonished I didn't shoot, and after a few seconds it flew up to the elm tree overhead – returning to try again, when I did shoot it. This was on beans, just after harvest, and perhaps adds weight to the well-held country theory that beans and peas inflame lust. When we were drilling peas, and I munched them from the drill box, the horseman would say: 'Do you keep a eaten them peas an' you'll hev to find a gel afore Sat'day,' continuing kindly to say which of the village girls would be most likely to give relief. Ducks' eggs were supposed to have the same randy effect.

But best of all traditional aphrodisiacs was the scent of the bean flower, for this not only stimulates passion in the man but extreme willingness in the girl. The frustrated lover was always told 'take har into the bin field, boy, and if there's a thorn bush or a bit of barbed wire, back har up agin it and she'll keep a' comen forrard to ye'. There was never any shortage of advice, either on how to get the girl, or how to avoid the consequences. 'Do you draw out on the hidland afore you tu'n the seed on, old mate, an' you'll be all right' – pious hopes which have persisted in the face of much evidence to the contrary! With most men, the talk, whenever it was about women, was always bawdy: no girl walking by escaped comment and speculation, and any younger chap who might have been seen talking to her would be closely questioned. 'Here, Harry, is that right you took har round the back of the [parish] room last dance?' Harry smirked, and kicked a clod in embarrassment 'Is that right she've got pink drawers?' But Harry is learning the way to get best in these exchanges – 'No, mate, that ain't, she don't wear none!' Whereupon we all laugh and say: 'The randy young tup!'

Perhaps because they had talked so loosely to their mates about young women of the village, their wives seemed cut off from conversation with any but their husbands. This was the general rule: you passed the time of day with other men's wives but nothing more – lest it should be thought you were wanting to improve on earlier speculation. I never even learned the first name of a single married woman in the whole time I was a pupil: and of the unmarried ones there is no need to speak. Nor in that time did I ever go into any of the cottages or any neighbouring farmhouses: social intercourse was restricted to the pub, the parish room very rarely and the fields. Occasionally the women would visit each other if their cottages were close, but not the men. They would stand in each other's gardens of a Sunday morning and discuss potatoes, but except in the case of illness they kept themselves to themselves. Farmers largely did likewise, meeting only at market or at sales.

Chapter Fourteen

FARM sales are normally held at Michaelmas or Lady Day, but during my time at the Home Farm there was scarcely a week when the Guv'nor didn't go to one or more. Every farmer was in debt. They owed their landlords, who no longer expected their rents on time and were glad if they got them at all. They owed merchants for seed, feed, and steam coal, and paid after harvest if there was anything to pay with. They owed the Tithe Commission which had less heart than merchants or landlords. And, of course, they owed the Banks. Some long-pursed merchants made a good thing out of owner-occupiers, allowing them to get hopelessly in debt, and then taking their farms over and sitting on them till better times came, leaving the dispossessed to join the long files of unemployed at the Labour Exchanges.

It was a terrible period to be farming: everything was going down hill. Arable land tumbled down to speargrass, bracken and brambles; buildings fell about the livestock's ears. Ditches and drains slowly filled, gutters fell, hedges grew tall and wide; only game and rabbits fattened. The smaller landlords were in almost as bad a plight as their tenants – their manor houses and halls lost roof-tiles which were not put back, their gravelled drives grew grass; park rails rusted, and scrubby animals roamed among ragwort and thistles and docks, where before fine pedigree cattle had grazed well-kept pastures. A few wealthy city men, seeing an opportunity to acquire cheap shooting, bought up large estates on the poor light lands – thousands of acres at as little as thirty bob an acre – and just grew enough arable crops to feed the pheasants they bred. Labourers here became under-keepers or poachers, or both – and counted themselves fortunate to have a job at all. The dispossessed farmers, no one wanted. Who would employ a man accustomed to command, in a menial capacity? So, for one reason and another, thousands of farmers went bust, and their land and live- and dead stock came under the auctioneer's hammer.

Sometimes I went with the Guv'nor. He would park the motor on the edge of the field among the dealers' carts and lorries and the tethered ponies of the small men, the poultry buyers and higglers, and walk over to where the dead stock was laid out in lines across a meadow by the buildings. Lots one to twenty had no interest for him. *Heap of firewood . . . Five empty barrels . . . Heap of old iron . . . Quantity of corn sacks . . . Quantity of galvanized iron sheeting . . . Half a dozen hen coops . . . Six ditto . . . Six ditto . . . Quantity of old harness.* The Guv'nor would pause at this lot to see if there was anything which might come in handy: a dutfin perhaps, or a collar with enough service in it to last a month or two without repairs. Then the hand tools. *Six muck forks . . . Three hay forks and a barley fork* (a three-tined fork used for loose barley) *. . . Potato skuvver and beet fork . . . Three hoes and an old stack knife . . . One cavings fork and drain tools.*

I never knew at all what the Guv'nor was looking for. He didn't want anyone to know – since, if they did,

it might cost him another shilling in the bidding. So he stuck the testing-point of his knife into the knave, spokes and felloes of each wheel on each cart and wagon, peered into the dusty innards of threshing drums, turned harrows on their backs and looked at their points, checked the serial numbers on plough shares – and gave no more hint of what he was really wanting until the bidding started. Even then it was hard to discover whether he was bidding or not. Cap well down over his nose, hands on his braces, expression unchanging, he simply stood, and by scarcely visible twitches informed the auctioneer that he was 'in'.

One sale I remember particularly well. It was almost on the Essex borders and farther away than the Guv'nor usually travelled. But the owner was an old threshing client of his, and since he was in fact being sold up (by

95

direction of the tithe owners) and would never farm again, this had something in the nature of a ceremonial farewell about it. On the way the Guv'nor told me about him: how he had started as a young man in 1900 with two sons and a hundred and fifty acres; how the army had taken both sons in the war; how he had struggled through the war and after that through the depression of the early twenties. Hard-working, straight, but never out of debt. It was a tale which was true of thousands. Two dry years – poor corn crops and poorer prices – and he was finished. The sale itself was also like so many others: a long list of lots in the early part of the catalogue; the broken-handled tools, old sacks and torn stack-covers; a very few useable implements, and these worn and old; and to finish – the horses. And this is why that sale is so memorable.

There were four Suffolks – two mares and two geldings – and they were sold last of all. The crowd, as usual, formed a long avenue thirty feet apart, with the auctioneer at one end. The first horse was brought out. The horseman handed the lead rein to the auctioneer's man at the stable door, and he with a crack of his long whip fast-trotted the animal to the end of the avenue, turned and came back with more whip-cracking to the auctioneer. Poor beast – I don't suppose it had had a whip near it since it was broken. It had been schooled *not* to gallop, *not* to charge around, but to proceed gently and quietly; and here was a strange man cutting the air and its flanks and demanding a charge between these rows of strangers. Meantime the auctioneer was telling the tale. 'First of the horses, gentlemen, Tommy, a strong gelding . . . plenty of work in him, sound feet, warranted in all gears, what will you say . . . Thirty guineas? . . . twenty then . . . Worth every penny, gentlemen . . . put me in, then . . .' Someone called out 'Ten', and in a few minutes the animal was knocked down at fifteen. Since the Guv'nor was not buying horses (this much I did know), I wandered off to the stables, where the next horse, the mare Dapper, was standing, ready to be taken out. The horseman, solemn in his best corduroys and Sunday cap, stood back holding the leading rein, and at the mare's head stood the farmer, with tears streaming down his face, stroking the animal's neck.

This little scene lasted only a few moments, but the impression it made on me will last for ever. Here was a man utterly crushed by economic forces he had no understanding of or control over. I had seen him earlier talking to farmers in the crowd: quiet, sad, self-possessed. The sale of harrows and harness, cultivators and chaff-cutter, had apparently left him unmoved; but the horses were different. Parting with these meant not only losing good friends, the companions of countless journeys up and down the fields; but with them the heart of the farm. No horses, no farming. I asked the Guv'nor what he would do now, and he told me he thought there was a brother the far side of the county who had a small place and would probably give him house-room. Maybe the brother would have, but he didn't; for two weeks later his wife found him hanging, dead, in an out-house. We heard about it from one of the threshing chaps, and the Guv'nor had Georgy clean the car and went to the funeral.

A length of rope over a beam in the barn, a charge of shot from a four-ten, a cold death in the horse pond;

how many farmers took these ways out? – and how many more lived with the fear that they, too, might be driven the same way? The men, particularly the older ones, were in even crueller plight. If their employers 'gave up' or were sold up, and no new man came in to take over the farm, or coming in required fewer hands, they had the workhouse to go to. Fear of the workhouse was as real and immediate as it ever had been – and like their masters many men took a short cut and put an end to it all.

Of course, I was only half-aware of what was in either the Guv'nor's or the men's minds. Everything was new to me, everything was exciting, and there was so much to take in and learn and be doing there was no time for speculation. These things and youth insulated me from realizing what a nightmare time it was for everyone.

Sales were always social, as well as business, occasions; people met to exchange news and gossip about other farmers and their crops. The dealers, moving from one sale to another, acted like mobile information bureaux, collecting news true and false and letting it fall casually in between bids and after the sale in the local to anyone interested. What with attendance at sales and the gossip brought home from outlying districts by the threshing men, the Guv'nor was particularly well-informed about what was going on. Within a few days of any 'new' man taking on a farm he would know where he came from, what his father did, who he was married to, whether he drank or gambled or ran after women, and – most important – how well-lined his breeches-pockets were. Yet I never heard him ask a direct question on such matters. The picture was built up from many angles – a detail here from one source, a missing piece from another – until it acquired almost three-dimensional roundness.

The Suffolk man likes to know but hates to ask, and will go to extraordinary and ingenious lengths to avoid the blunt question. For instance, if a threshing contractor heard that a farmer had a Ransome's drum he wanted to sell and which the contractor wanted to buy, he would approach him sideways by asking him whether it was true that some third party had (as he had heard) a Bentall's for sale – adding that he didn't particularly want a Bentall, preferring a Clayton. If the farmer did really want to sell his drum, he would then have to disclose the fact and state that it was a Ransome, which then allowed the contractor to make a very low offer – since he had already said it was a Clayton he was looking for. And, supposing the contractor had merely been satisfying his curiosity, this conversation had value since he had turned a second-hand piece of information into a first-hand one. 'You can take it from me that's right – I was talking to him the other day and he told me himself he wanted to sell his drum.' This is no longer gossip – it is a fact and straight from source – which is perhaps why, if you come fresh to a place in Suffolk, you will be asked questions to which the inquirer already knows the answers – but don't forget that it is shocking bad manners to suggest you know he knows.

Auctioneers are different. They are professionally licensed to ask direct questions and licensed, too, to put their own construction on your answers, which is how the gelding Tommy, aged fifteen, becomes 'Tommy'; a 'valuable gelding warranted sound and quiet in all gears' or Sarah, an ancient cow of indeterminate breed which none the less happens to be in calf, becomes '*Sarah, deep milking Shorthorn cow, near to profit*'. Not that anyone who matters was ever taken in by an auctioneer's description; the ringside worthies, on remarking the signs of age in the cow, would probably call out, 'Here's one for the dog-meat man', or, if any hunting fellow was among the onlookers, they would call to him, 'Don't you buy it, Guv'nor – chance you'll hev her cheaper termorrow' – meaning the cow would be dead by then and the hunt kennels would get it for a few shillings. Auctioneers were (and are) different, too, in that their money is secure. They remove their commission from receipts before paying the seller his due; so that, notwithstanding depressions, they do all right. Barring drink – an occupational hazard – and speculation in property at the wrong time, they never go bust.

At the end of one sale the auctioneer came up to me: 'I hear you're pupil at Home Farm, young man.' – 'Yes, that's right, I am.' – 'Couldn't be at a better place, nor with a better farmer – you'll learn, I can see that.' – I murmured, 'Yes, I hoped so.' – 'A lot of people would say you are wrong to be going in for farming just now. Things are very low – look at that binder I just sold – seven-fifteen, and damn near new – worth thirty and last a lifetime. Of course, things *are* down – no one can deny it'. – I didn't try. – 'But isn't that the very best time *to* start farming? Think of the capital you can *save* going in now!' I said I reckoned he was right. He moved forward a foot and inclined his head confidentially to my ear. 'Now, look here, young man, I won't beat about the bush. You know the tenant here is

100

going out – well, this is a tidy farm, good land, buildings not bad, and if you can show me a thousand
pound . . .' On seeing my vacant look, he changed this
to five hundred. 'If you can show me five hundred
pound in the bank, you can have this farm – two
hundred acres – for three years rent free. Rent nego-
tiated at the end of that time, and' – he went on – 'if
you could raise another few hundred, I expect the
owner would let you have the Hill End farm on the
same conditions as well – I'll speak to him for you.'

I was flattered – oh, how I was flattered! Seventeen
years old, less than twelve months' experience, and here
was this man – this knowledgeable man of the agricultural world – suggesting I would make a good tenant
for two or three hundred acres of tender Suffolk loam –
and that I might have a thousand pounds locked up in
the bank to boot. From that moment on I felt slightly
taller and a lot wider, and can only believe it was
some vestigial Scots caution which kept me from even
attempting to take up his offer. Had I done so – had I
raised sufficient wind – it would probably have taken
me less than those three years to discover that rent-free
farms are not the most profitable. But the auctioneer
would have sold me implements and made a bit that
way, and the landlord (who, not finding a tenant,
would have had to 'farm' it himself) would have had
me there to keep the land in shape and save it from
utter ruin.

Later on I was offered other farms under similar
conditions – it is a commentary on the times. Given a
clear head, a little money and enough experience, it
could have worked. Those who did go into farming
with enough of these, and lasted out until 'thirty-seven

or 'thirty-eight when the tide turned, found themselves well-off by the late 'forties; and, if they happened to have *bought* land in the 'thirties and managed to hang on, then they became really rich. But only if they converted land into money, for since 1955 the returns on capital invested in farming have become progressively smaller.

At seventeen, thoughts like these were still far from my mind. Phrases such as 'return on capital invested' were not current among farmers then, and my head was too full of rich and satisfying practical things to have much room for such abstract matters. Indeed, I doubt whether at that time I ever considered the *future* at all; each day was an adventure in itself, and there seemed no reason why succeeding days should not be the same. This does not mean I enjoyed all days equally: some, indeed, I disliked and even feared − threshing, for instance, or riddling potatoes in a sleeting north-easter without protection for nine hours on end. But bitter cold, wet feet, or the prickly sweating days of barley harvest, when awns ('avels' we called them) embedded themselves in your navel and scratched your neck, wrists and waist raw, these were new experiences: to be a man, you had to know how to put up with them. The spur was to be as strong and skilled as the chaps − to be one of them. So far as money goes, on five shillings a week and keep I was probably − no, certainly − better off than the married men. Clothes were cheap, and tobacco, one ounce a week smoked with a drying throat and sore tongue, cheap enough too. Black Shag wrapped in a twist of paper, Red Indian Chief, Blue Bell and Roll Call − marvellous to smell from someone else's pipe on a frosty morning, but like fumes from a coke fire when drawn from mine. Cough, cough, choke and splutter: 'Ah boy, that's man's terbacca, that is. Don't corf so, you'll frighten the hosses!'

It's all right now looking back and calculating how in 1935 you could go into a pub and buy an ounce of tobacco, a box of matches and a pint of beer all for a shilling — but for the married man with kids there wasn't the shilling to do it with. I managed fine, and even bought a pair of handsome riding breeches, very wide, stiff and with well-stuck-out sides, rather like wings on the thigh. These must have been fashionable, but the chaps — Walter, I think it was — said: 'There he go — two penn'orth of shirt, and a bob's worth of backside in a quid's worth of breeches, and no horse under 'em.' I fancied myself in those togs and thought him a vulgar fellow — which he was. But right in his sense of proportion. A pound was more than he would pay for trousers or breeches, more than he could afford; and why should a green pupil still wet behind the ears think well of himself because of his breeches?

Unlike the rest of the horsemen, Walter was noisy and unpredictable and a bit bad tempered. 'Hev you se'n Walter this mornen?' — 'No, I hent, but d'you listen 'n you'll hear him a' thoshen his horses up and down Old Field!' You could hear him fields away, cursing and swearing at his horses, the plough, the land, and (when he was at home), at his wife and squads of children. His wife had a tongue, too, and for a Suffolk woman was extremely outspoken, accusing him in public of having ungovernable lusts. I think they were fond of each other, and the children looked up to him as a god — perhaps because he knew more bad language than they did. On the whole, the farm did not approve.

We may have thought children of tender years a bloody nuisance, but would not have spoken of our own as young buggers — it was not done. When they grew to man's estate — say, fifteen — it became all right, but not before.

Chapter Fifteen

W HAT happened to haysel during my time at Home Farm – or what I was otherwise engaged in – I have no idea. There is a faint recollection of helping to stack stover, but quite likely I confuse it with another farm. There was probably very little hay made, anyway, since it was a drought year and grass grew woefully sparse – and, come to think of it, we were doing quite a lot of hedging and flashing out of brews and ditches during what should have been a busy hay time.

Harvest, my first harvest, is not forgotten. Towards the end of July Georgy and I were put to looking over the wagons while George and the Guv'nor went to work on the binders. The wagons were old; their bottoms had been patched until hardly any original planking was left. Their wheels needed the pond treatment, and a nail or two to hold the iron tyres to the felloes. Yet despite their condition they had a classical beauty about them, with the long sweeping line from the slightly tilted front lade to the finality of the back lade, the bold voluting on the short uprights of the buck, and the strong but delicately-twisted iron work supporting the side rails, on (to give them their proper name) raves. With a good Suffolk punch in the shafts and another in the traces, they had a statuesque nobility and were truly a monument to the skill of the horse breeders and wheelwrights who evolved them. Incidentally, hitch a tractor to one of these old wagons and observe how it diminishes the tractor to a here-today-and-gone-tomorrow upstart vulgarity. To compare a wagon built around the turn of the century (which is what ours were) with today's trailers, is like comparing an Old Master with an art school abstract. They were built by old masters of their craft. To ride, sitting on the side rails, as they bumped over the fields was akin to being in a well-found fishing boat – perfectly designed for its purpose.

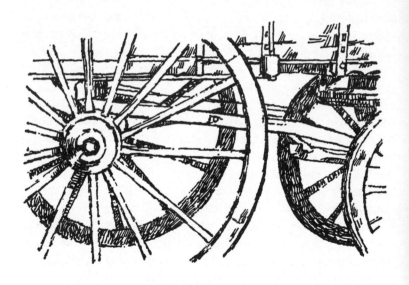

George and the Guv'nor had a long discussion about whether the binder-canvasses needed re-splining through-out; but in the end, and having pulled down from the loft a collection of almost equally tatty ones bought at sales, they decided to patch them up – to put a few new rivets in, sew on one or two patches and hope for the best. Binders are uncomfortable bits of machinery; from the simple cast-iron seat which, unless cushioned with a straw-filled bag, left a deep and complicated imprint of the maker's name on your backside, to the more complex moving parts of the knotter. The knotter (or so we believed) was perfected by a Canadian, who, when he had completed his work, committed suicide because he didn't understand why it worked. Many a farm worker and farmer since then has certainly been driven nearly mad by generations of knotters, and even now, after all these years, I sheer off from them like a young horse from a traction engine. George was 'good with knotters', and with a bent screw-driver and a wobbly adjustable spanner made them work so that they turned out sheaves neat and uniform and fit for harvest festival; the string or bond tight but not too tight, the knot firm, and the butt ends packed sloping and neat, so they would stand in the traves without too much clapping of the ears together or pressing of the butts into the land.

I actually started work in the harvest field a week after the first wheats were cut and traved. I was to help in the carting. Willy had laid out a bottom of bean straw to the dimensions he thought would hold the field – a seven-acre piece – and was in charge at the stackyard end. George was in charge of carting, the field end of operations.

I rode down in one of the wagons to the field where the traves were 'aisled' and waiting. Once through the gate the head dayman, Fred, called out: 'Hey, George, we aren't working with this young chap here, not till

107

he've bin shod and paid his footing' – 'Tha's right,' answered George. 'Do you collar him and we'll see to that job now.' Whereupon the daymen collared me firmly, tripped me up and sat on my chest, while one of the others grabbed hold of my feet. George then came up with a hammer taken from the binder-box and smartly hammered the soles of my boots until I hollered for mercy. Then, when they let me go and I got to my feet, wondering what on earth this was all about, the men stood round in a ring and, at a word from George, all shouted at the top of their voices, 'He's shod! – He's shod – The colt is shod!' 'And now', said George, 'you've got to pay your footing – a gallon of beer'll do.' Unhappily, I hadn't a penny on me, but George lent me two and eightpence and sent one of Walter's boys off to the pub with it – Walter cuffing the boy as he went – 'And don't you go suppin' it on the way back! do, I'll tan your young arse fer you.' So I was formally initiated and given the freedom of the harvest field. It was a custom which had gone on for centuries – exactly how long no one knows – but I do know I was the last to be shod at Home Farm, and quite possibly the last in England, for in most places it had died out during the First World War. There was *talk* about shoeing the colt after that, but it was never actually done again.

Carting was organized in teams. Each team had two wagons and two horses and a boy to drive away, and one or two loaders, with two pitchers to each, so the chaps on the load had a steady flow of sheaves forked up to them which they then laid by hand. In that part, for some reason, forks were not used on the loads at all. I was put to load with one of the under horsemen and from him took instruction in the art. And it was an art.

First, the buck had to be filled with sheaves laid over-lapping so as to provide a solid base. Then a layer round the outside, butts out and sticking well beyond the raves, and the same on the front and back lades. Next a layer of 'binders' – sheaves set with their butts extending only as far out as the strings round the first layer. Then another layer to bind the binders, and so on until the middle of the load was reached and the sheaves over-lapped from both sides and ends. That made one course. The next and succeeding courses were made in the same way, until the load looked like a miniature stack on wheels.

At the tail of each wagon hung a wagon rope. One looped end was hooked on to the underside of the wagon and the other thrown over the load; before the rope was fastened we used it to slide down. My loads needed the rope, but the best men would lay their sheaves so perfectly that they would ride over the roughest ground. Corners were my trouble: it was easy enough to learn how to bind the sheaves along the sides of the load, but the corners were much more difficult, since one sheaf on the extreme corner could obviously not have its next fellow in line with it. On two occasions my ends of the loads were so doubtful that, even with a rope on, George would not allow them to leave the field. There and then, they were dissected and rebuilt. As each load was completed, the boy with the empty wagon transferred the trace-horse to the full one and led it away to the stack. Walter seemed to supply most of the boys – tough kids from seven to twelve, but already strong and confident. They walked at the thil horse's head, driving the trace-horse with a plough line and almost trotting to keep up with them. Through narrow gateways, across the main road, down the lane and up into the stackyard, where they drew up alongside the building stack.

This first field was wheat – Little Joss – and as the straw was long it was easy to load. Being with a gang of experienced men, I soon got in the swing of it. There is a wonderful rhythm about corn carting. The pitcher puts his fork into a sheaf and swings it up to the loader in such a way that it comes to hand for placing just where it is needed. The loader doesn't want to have to turn round and look for the sheaf; he expects it to arrive in the right place at the right time and the right way round, so it does not have to be turned either. That sheaf delivered, and the next one is on its way, until the trave is finished. The horseman shouts 'hold tight', by way of warning, and the horse without further prompting moves on between the next pair of traves. A good, well trained horse would judge when the trave was opposite the wagon and stop of his own accord, but sometimes they would stop too soon and the pitcher would say, 'Jist-step, just a step, old hoss,' and he would move on a few paces.

I found loading by hand hard work. It wasn't too bad with wheat sheaves, but the lighter barley sheaves flew up at such a rate from the forks of the pitchers I could hardly keep pace. And the barley avels teased my unaccustomed skin cruelly, crawling up my sleeves, into my neckband and round my waist, setting up a screaming irritation. There were thistles, too, and in a bad field hands became so full of prickles that you could hardly put a pin between them. By way of warning, when a particularly bristling sheaf was coming up, the pitchers would shout 'Jacobites!' – a term I have never

110

heard anywhere else and which no one has ever been able to explain to me. Had it, I wonder, something to do with Scotland – the Scottish Thistle? – and, if so, why should it appear here in Suffolk? But names – nicknames – stick for small reasons, and persist for years after their origins are lost. One field I know of, which appears on maps as 'Square Field' and was such for generations, became Canary Field, not because any canary ever flew there but because it was planted during the war with canary seed. That was twenty-five years ago. It is still called Canary Field, and the old name is gone, perhaps for ever. The new one may last a century – or die in a decade.

It is not always the old men who remember the old names: children can become repositories – as a friend of mine found in the village where he had farmed all his life. Outside the Junior School one day he was almost knocked over by a ten-year-old boy on a bicycle. 'Where do you think you are going?' – 'I'm going to race Sam to the Red Gate.' – 'Red Gate? – where's that?' – 'Up the road, round the corner past the cottages' – 'Oh . . . you mean the Black Gate.' – 'No, I don't. The Black Gate is on the other side of the road – the Red Gate is the next one on the left.' Now every-one in the village knows where the Black Gate is, even though no gate of any colour whatever has swung on the post for twenty or thirty years. Come to that, there's no post there, either. The conversation went on. 'There isn't any gate on the left.' – 'No, I know there ain't, but there's a gateway and that's the Red Gate.' – 'Well, if there isn't any gate, why do you call it the Red Gate?' – 'Oh, I don't know, we just call it that.' And off he cycled. Puzzled by this, my friend asked all the old men of the village if they knew where the Red Gate was, but it was only when he asked his pensioner pigman that he got the answer. 'Yes, when I was a nipper I recollect my old dad sending me to pick up his frail [bag] as he left hang'n on a stub by the Red Gate, an' I asked *him* why it was called the Red Gate. He told me that when *he* was a boy there was an old gate there, and it had been red – but it had been broken and taken away 'fore he left school.' That meant there had been no gate there for a century – yet the school children, or some of them, knew where it was although their parents and even grandparents did not. It seems as though the knowledge was passed from child to child at school, and forgotten by them when they left. What is even stranger about this story is that the little boy whom my friend first quizzed was an American, the son of an airman stationed in Suffolk.

Since you can cart wheat when it is still damp with dew, those first days of carting were long ones: the heat from the sun which had risen in cloudless skies and went down in a hot red heat-haze, the itching, the thirst, made eight o'clock come none too soon. Walter's boy brought out the last empty wagon, and hitching the trace horse on to ours drove home while we lounged at ease on top of the swaying load. I thought then, and still think, there is no better way of finishing a day's work – lying on your back looking up through the branches of overhanging trees, insulated by ten feet of corn sheaves from the shock of iron tyres on a rough lane. Peace, perfect peace, and tomorrow far away!

George did all the cutting – except the swathe round

the headlands, which was done by a couple of odd chaps with scythes to make room for the machine and horses. George worked long hours whenever the corn was fit, starting with Willy's pair of horses and changing over in early afternoon to his own. A boy would take his change team to the field for him, or, if there was water in the field, George took both pairs and their nose-bags. The Guv'nor liked to have his corn traved right behind the binder, so that should the weather turn wet the sheaves would be standing and shed the worst of the water. It is remarkable how much water a well-made trave will shed – they look so vulnerable to rain. What they can't put up with is long periods of rain and muggy weather, when the grain begins to put out shoots and then roots, so the heads of the sheaves grow together in a tangled mass of white root fibres and green shoots. But this was a fine year – we had no trouble from wet worth speaking of.

As George went round and round, and the area of standing corn grew smaller, the rabbits began to run from it, and we chaps traving would run after them. Men whom I had never seen move faster than a loping walk suddenly became boys again and hallooing and whistling hared off after the dodging rabbits until they either escaped to the hedge or took refuge under a fallen sheaf. If this happened the man hurled himself bodily onto it, putting his arms round it, nipping in his elbows close to the sides of the sheaf and imprisoning the rabbit, then to be dragged out and with a quick pull have its neck dislocated. Sometimes, on fields where the rabbit infestation was likely to be very thick, the Guv'nor would post me at one corner, the keeper at another and maybe a friend and the Guv'nor himself at the remaining two – all armed with twelve-bores and orders not to miss. I think the keeper – to whom rabbit shooting brought no profit – really came to see no pheasants or hares were shot. One afternoon four of us went to a twelve-acre field of wheat, which George had started cutting earlier. We ran out of cartridges while there was still half an acre standing, and when George finally stopped the binder at the end of the last strip, he pulled seventeen rabbits from under the bottom canvas where they had run. From that twelve acres we killed over two hundred rabbits with two hundred and thirty cartridges. Hulking and hurdling took an age, and in the end I think most of them were buried, since the price in the market wasn't enough to pay the transport.

On that day the keeper was an understrapper – more of an estate warrener, really – and distinguished by the most villainous squint I have ever seen. This did not prevent him from being a remarkable shot – but I shall not forget my uncomfortable feeling when, looking at me, he raised his gun and shot a rabbit at ninety degrees between us. I damn near died of fright! We were always warned about not shooting too close to the binder. There were dreadful warnings from men who had seen horses stung with pellets bolt with binder and driver through too narrow a gateway, with the result that the binder was smashed, the horses ruined and the driver injured. Another hazard for the binder driver was wasps' nests. I once saw George fighting to control his team when they had been stung almost to madness by wasps whose nest the bull wheel had passed over. George won that battle, but got badly stung himself. Children, too, could be a hazard, though more to themselves than to horses or men. The Guv'nor stood no nonsense from excited juvenile rabbit-catchers. 'Go on, off you go, keep to the headland, or out of it altogether' – and they did. There was a case in the next parish, though, where a young horseman watching a whole gang of men chasing a rabbit failed to notice a small boy standing in the corn and in the path of his binder. How it happened I cannot imagine, but the sails knocked the child clear of the knife and onto the bottom canvas: this carried him to the elevator canvasses, which in turn delivered him to the packers and knotter; and from thence, tied with a nicely knotted bond of binder twine round his middle, he was dropped to the ground. Somewhat scared I would say, but otherwise unharmed. Others less fortunate had feet or hands severed – but not in my time in that area: we saw reports in the papers which the Guv'nor read aloud by way of warning to learners.

After a week or so carting – both pitching and loading – the Guv'nor sent me to the stackyard for a change. And what a change in the scenery there! What had been a nettle-grown yard, with the fag-ends of hay and straw stacks looking derelict, unused and uncared for, was now transformed into the centre of the farm's activity. First I was put to unloading the wagons and soon learned why it was important they should be loaded according to the rule. Unloading became simply the reverse process. The last sheaf on top was the first onto the stack, and then one merely followed the courses round and round and down and down until the last one had gone, the empty wagon was drawn away, and a full one replaced it. When the stack was young and low, unloading was easy – all downhill work. But one was expected to maintain the same rate of unloading whatever the height, and when this meant pitching up higher than fork length it was tiring, but the pressure from fresh wagons arriving kept one at it. Just as with pitching to wagon loaders, pitching to the man on the stack had to be accurate: each sheaf presented longways on with the butt pointing in the direction of the stacker's mate or feeder, so that he could catch it and pass it to the stacker without having to fumble or turn it in the process. The stacker's mate had to watch out since as the stacker moved round the direction of his throw must alter, and the presentation of the sheaf by the unloader had to change likewise. Again, it was a marvellous rhythm of swinging forks to the accompaniment of rustling straw and the patter of loose grain falling on it. As the stack rose higher, a third man was needed to feed the mate, so they pulled a sheaf or two from about eaves-level, and he remained in that place until the stack was completed. This meant, too, that the unloader had a fixed place to throw to. This eaves-level spot was known as the bully hole, and with hob-nailed boots on fresh, slippery wheat-stalks it could be dangerously slippery. Besides that, once in it you stayed there, which meant pitching all the time up and behind your back to the roof above. Sometimes, when the Guv'nor for some reason wanted a much larger stack than usual, or decided to put another field of corn on a stack with a bottom designed for a smaller acreage, another man would be added to the team and another bully hole made a fork's length above the first. The resulting stack would be a monument, would have a great towering roof, and take the thatcher days to cover.

If Willy (who was, of course, stacking) couldn't see

the field from the stack, he would tell the boys driving away to ask the carters how many loads were left in the field, so that he could draw in the roof slower or faster accordingly. As the last few courses on the roof approached, he would shout down to ask how much was left on the load, and then, if it was the last load, 'Give us a shout when you git t' the raves, boy!'; so that the sheaves left in the buck could be made to finish the ridge of the stack. It did not always work out quite exactly, and if perhaps needing a few more he would send word to the carting team for so many courses of rough headland sheaves to finish off with. If any were left over, they went on the bottom of the next stack. Willy was brilliant at his job. He would come down maybe twice in a day (other than at meal times) and walk round his creation just giving a bit of a shove to a jutting sheaf or pulling a corner sheaf out a fraction. He seemed to know without looking what was happening, and he had the rare ability of building a stack on sloping ground which would not tilt as it settled. The chaps were all agreed – 'Blast, yes, old Willy's the hid chap fer stacking – there aren't nobody as can raise 'em up same as he can – an' he don't hev to go roun' with the clippers to tidy 'em up after, neither.' His was an art and a science. Think of the variable factors – the length of straw, the weight of ears, the kind of cereal, the way it was cut, and the lie of the land – and wonder that a man like Willy could compose from them stacks of uniform size, if required, so well built that they would settle evenly and their roofs throw off water almost without thatch. Consider this, and marvel. Marvel too, if you will, that he thought himself a lesser creature than a man doing repetition factory work, and grind

117

your teeth that the world is so organized that these skills, and those practised by his forebears and successors, have never been adequately paid for.

Not all stackers would allow a bully hole to be made, because it was difficult to fill in neatly without destroying the regular line of the eaves in the finished stack. To get over the difficulty, they had a 'monkey stage', which served the same purpose. This consisted of two stout ash poles eight foot long, set parallel and two or three feet apart, built into the stack at the required level, with about two foot left sticking out and tilting slightly upwards from the stack. On to these poles boards were nailed, making a little platform on which the third man would stand. Then, when the stack was finished, the poles were withdrawn and no patching was needed. It was all important at harvest time to get the work of carting and stacking geared correctly together. With two pitchers in the field, the unloader had to work at exactly twice their pace or keep them waiting for wagons. Since they lost time moving from trave to trave, and in hitching and unhitching, this was quite possible – but there was no time to waste. And it equally meant the stacker had to lay his sheaves fast. However, except for the corners and towards the eaves and the ridge, all of which needed extra skill, his feeder would follow round working inside and slightly behind, binding the stacker's row – so that the stacker only handled alternate sheaves. Then, while the stacker was doing the tricky bits and outside courses, his mate would pass on an even smaller proportion, putting the rest towards the middle of the stack. The call was always, 'Keep your middle full!' – so that all sheaves tilted away from the middle and towards the outside.

118

This ensured a full roof, and one which would not go hollow backed. Moreover, should the thatch come adrift, the tilt on the sheaves would still to a great extent shoot the rain off, and prevent it dribbling down and spoiling the lot. We never used an elevator at the stack while I was there. I think the Guv'nor would have liked to, but Willy was against it, I suspect, and his wishes had to be considered.

That harvest was a wonderful one. Not for yields of corn, since, good or bad, they made no difference to me; but for the experience of being part of a sweetly running organization which at every stage of operations changed the landscape, leaving it dramatically different yet still beautiful. From standing corn to fallen sheaves, from the long aisles of traves to the bare biscuit-coloured stubbles, it was a royal progress, which, because of the weight of tradition behind it, the unwritten rules and its *inevitability*, had a formality at the same time grandly impressive and warmly intimate. The days of the harvest 'Lord' were already past, though the men often talked of the times when, for the season, the 'Lord' was as important as the farmer himself. I suppose George acted as the Lord inasmuch as he bargained with the Guv'nor on the men's behalf about the amount they would 'take the harvest' for. That year it was seven pounds ten. At the end of harvest each man received that sum but no payment for overtime on harvest work during the period. It was understood that the hours worked would be reasonable, and that year anyway there were no upsets.

Naturally, I worked the same hours as everyone else, but I did not get harvest money, though on one occasion I did come in for extra payment in the shape of beer. It happened that all the men were in one field at the same time. Willy and his gang were getting a stack bottom ready, the wagons and their attendants were just starting to get the first loads, and the odd men, me among them, were opening out to the sun a few traves which, from being deep in the shade of overhanging trees, had become damp. The Guv'nor's motor edged through the gateway and stopped by the stack. He had a man with him, a stranger – and one of the older men tramping the stack-bottom and seeing him raised the cry 'Largesse, largesse!' which was taken up by everyone in earshot. Even Walter's little boys were hollering 'Largesse' at the top of their voices. The stranger – and by stranger, I mean someone who was not ordinarily seen on the farm – knew what was expected of him – he put his hand in his pocket and, walking over to Willy, presented him with enough silver, ten shillings or so, to buy a quart of beer all round. Walter's eldest was sent off for it at once and at bait time the jug went round. I came to the conclusion that it depended upon the size of the stranger's response to the cry of 'Largesse!' whether he could be described as a decent sort of man, a gentleman, or a *real* gentleman. That year, despite the low cost of acquiring the status, *real* gentlemen were few and far between. But strangely enough, although the beer was important to us, I got the feeling that it was not primarily for beer that the cry of 'Largesse' was raised, but rather that a tradition should be honoured in the time-honoured manner. Largesse may have been a gratuity, but it was also a right, and had nothing of a tip about it: it could be called for in a loud voice without loss of dignity. Alas, along with 'shoeing the colt', the practice is long since

120

dead. You might holler 'Largesse!' from the seat on a combine at the top of your voice, but no one could hear you – and if they did, they would not know what the hell you were shouting about.

Harvest finished very early – mid-September – which augured ill for yields. The Guv'nor bit his lip as he walked round the stacks: there were not enough of them. But for the men it was a welcome end since it came on a Saturday, and both the week's money and the harvest money would be paid at the same time. The last full load rolled up to the last stack, followed by a part-load and an empty wagon with the men sitting on the raves: the young ones singing 'All is safely gathered in', but with new and highly improper words which faded into slightly shame-faced silence as the Guv'nor joined them with his long leather money bag. And that was that. 'See you at the White Hoss – don't let yar missus hev it all . . . blast, we've wholly earnt a pint or two!'

Chapter Sixteen

FOR about six weeks before and after Christmas I went to plough. Perhaps the Guv'nor felt things were running behind schedule, or perhaps he thought I should have the experience; but whichever it was (probably a bit of both) I am still grateful, for this was the crowning experience of my whole pupillage at Home Farm. Six o'clock in the stables: we are finished feeding and grooming, and ready harnessed the horses stand at the manger, blowing the last few oats from the chaff, while we wait for George to give the signal to start. Inside the stable, warm, the rounded backsides of the horses softly shining in the light of the hurricane lamps; smells of dung, hay, horses and harness, and a whiff of forbidden tobacco smoke. The Guv'nor has stumped off back to the house. George pulls out his watch, 'Time we was off,' and calls to his pair, which are at the far end of the stable, to come to him: 'Blossom, cup-i-wi, hoss, Bowler, cup-i-wi.' They turn from the manger to the door where George waits and plunge out into the yard. The rest of us and our horses follow in turn, six men and six pairs, mine last.

Outside, it is still pitch-black and cold as we cross the yard and file out into the lane. We walk, each man at the shoulder of his nearside horse, one hand on dinner bag or plough chains looped from the hame-hook; no need to lead with the rein. Once on the hard road the

122

horses kick sparks from the metal, and our hobnails do the same, so that it is almost as if the stars shining from the black sky are reflected under foot. We keep close to our horses for the warmth they give off; no one speaks; just the clatter of hooves and boots, the occasional snort as the cold air bites stable-warm windpipes, and the wind shaking the bare branches of overhanging elms. Up the lane, past the cottages showing faint yellow candlelight behind closed curtains and fires already alight by the smell of woodsmoke. Still too dark to see the horses in front, but you can tell what is happening by the sounds. Big Boxer 'cops', with his off hind just catching the off fore shoe, Duchess picks her feet up quickly – more like a hackney than a cart horse – her shoes on the hard road sound as though she is about to break into a little dance, and you know her ears are pricked forward and her tail held high.

George turns his team from the road and into Kells – the field we are ploughing – and the noise of hooves changes from iron on road metal to the softer thud on packed earth. Through the gateway, turn left along the headland to where our cold-handled ploughs were left the day before. At this time of the morning at this time of the year there is no hurry to get hitched; take it easy, because it's still not light enough to start. Unhook my dinner bag from the hames and hang it in the hedge – don't leave it on the ground, because by bait time, as like as not, the rats would have it. I once opened my ex-army canvas bag at bait time, and out jumped two young rats and no fat left on the bacon! Then back the horses to the plough, unhook the looped plough chains hanging from the hame hooks and hook them on to the whippletrees, making sure the hooks are turned

123

inward, so they don't catch in turning. Then unloop the plough lines (never called reins), and, starting at the rings on the plough handles, thread them through, then through the rings on the back strap and, finally, to the bits.

Along the headland, the men moving about – 'Git over, Captain – git over, blast you . . .! Back a step, Duke . . . weurdi, old mare.' And Walter swearing – damning and blasting, bleeding and worse. 'Where's the ile can, Willy? My bloody land wheel'll shrik all day do I don't give it some ile.' – 'Tha's where you left it – with the hammer, again the oak stub.' George leaves his horses and walks over to see that I have hitched up properly. He looks at the lines and chains. 'I sh'd move the hake a snotch to the right – your furrow hoss dont pull quite so hard as the young 'un.' And he moves the chain, giving the furrow horse an advantage. Turning the plough on its side, he looks at the share. 'That'll do for today, but you want a new peg – do that'll come off next time you pull back.' He feels in his pocket and fetches out a short green oak peg, and, taking out the old one, replaces it with the new, hammering it in with the plough-spanner.

It is very still and cold as we wait for the light. I can hear the faint clatter of pails and the squeal of pigs in the distance: Georgy is feeding. The bull is complaining softly to himself from his pen by the cowshed: from the village a mile away the tiny tin trumpets of bantam cocks. Somewhere out in front a peewit gets up with a lonely-sounding cry and comes over close enough for its flapping wings to be heard – it swerves off with another call, which is answered from fields away. George says, 'Phoebe's late this morning! Are ye right,

Willy? We'd best be off . . . Git up, Bowler, Blossom, git up then.' I right my plough, grip the cold handles, shake the reins; the horses lean into their collars and take the strain; chains jangle taut and the plough enters the earth with a harsh scraping screek. The first furrow of the morning. By the time we are half-way across the field I can see all the teams, the sky is pale lemon and the dawn wind freshens cold, so I'm glad to be moving. Two more furrows, and it's broad daylight: the gulls, which have spent the night on the estuary a few miles away, have joined us and a small flock follows each plough, screaming and fighting for worms. They are hungry, but not so hungry they come too close, as they will in starvation weather when, catching a glimpse of a worm as the furrow turns, they sometimes get themselves ploughed in. With horses it is easy to stop and rescue them, but with a multi-furrow tractor plough the bird is probably killed, or trapped, half-buried by the weight of earth and dies of hunger, since the driver presses on, regardless.

There is nothing to match the pleasure of ploughing with a willing pair of horses and a Ransome's Y.L. plough. An iron plough, this implement was first manufactured in 1843 and even a hundred years later was still selling in big numbers. And no wonder, since it combined beauty with perfect utility. The earth flows like a wave from the long sweet curve of its breast, with minimum effort. It is so well balanced that once the wheels and hake were adjusted, with a steady pair of horses, you could let go the handles and it would ride by itself. We sometimes did this if we thought the Guv'nor was away. Another man and I would start our teams off from opposite ends of the field: he would turn my team at his end and I would turn his at mine, and send them back to each other. This was all right provided the horses kept going, but you felt an awful fool when they stopped mid-field and you had to walk over and restart them and then run back in time to turn the other pair. The Guv'nor was known to disapprove of the practice, so it was only when the coast was clear and George was in a benevolent mood and we felt skittish, that it ever happened.

Walking behind the plough, one hand on the plough handle, one on the plough-line, up and down, up and down, furrow after furrow, gradually changing pale sand-coloured wind-dry soil into a moist dark brown, broken texture. Hour after hour, day after day, and never for one moment bored: there is too much to think about and to notice. You can tell by the sound of the share in the soil where you are in the field. The gravelly stony patch is harsh and noisy, the wet patch makes a slithering noise, and in yet another belt, which stretches right across the field, the earth is soft and loamy, full of organic matter, and the plough goes silent. There are even subtle changes in the smell of the soil, but these are masked by the acrid sweat from the horses and smoke from a hedger's fire a field away. I think about what I'm doing: should I move the hake a snotch to the right or the cat's-head one peg down; is the wedge which should hold the land-wheel stalk firm in its socket coming loose? There are a score of details to watch for but when everything is going well my mind slides off into speculation. Perhaps this field has been under the plough off and on for three or four centuries; maybe longer. Ploughed by men in leather jerkins driving teams of oxen pulling crude wooden

126

ploughs, but using the same words we use. They would speak as we do of a 'fleet' furrow – a shallow one: with them, as with us, it would be a plough 'shear' rather than share, and rightly, since it does shear the furrow from the solid earth. George, Willy, Walter and the rest are all dressed in ex-army clothes – khaki breeches, old brass-buttoned tunics and great-coats from 1914. Some of the chaps even wear puttees – 'they wholly keep ya legs warm, bor'. Did those distant ploughmen wear the discarded uniforms of old wars, too? In my mind's eye I can see faded red coats, smocks with old heraldic markings, red jackets from the Crimea, from the Zulu wars. I knew of a retired professional boxer who bought a farm in Essex, just outside Colchester, and his wife sent him to plough in full evening dress. Why not . . . ? He wouldn't be eating dinner with the swells any more. With a mud-stained dickey and tails flying in the wind he was quite a sight, but a trifle incongruous, since on top he wore a bowler hat and on his feet heavy brown boots.

At ten o'clock George gives the signal for bait. We pull out on to the headland and set the ploughs in the next furrow to hold the horses while we eat. Dinner bags are pulled from the hedge, and we sit in a row, each on an old bag for protection from the damp earth. Madam has put me up cold bacon sandwiches, two rock buns and a bottle of cold tea with a smell of whisky about it. We all drink cold tea – vacuum flasks were about, but not on that farm. The chaps eat bread and cheese – big hunks of bread and not too much cheese, but with a good onion for relish. Food finished, we sit back, light pipes and talk. Talk, not of football or cinema or politics, but of land and crops and gardens

and village scandal – and horses, of course. Half an hour, and George looks at his watch; we take a last swig of cold tea, knock out pipes on the heels of our boots and go back to the ploughs – each man turning his on its side to look at the share before starting. And from then until half-past two or three in the afternoon we go up and down, finishing stetch after stetch until it is time to knock off. We leave the ploughs set upright in the ground looking like strange elegant sea-birds at rest, and the gulls replete with worms sit for a while on the last furrows and then, like us, take off for home.

Going home we ride. One foot in the looped plough chain, a hand on the wooden hame, and we heave ourselves up to sit half on and half off the pad. No need to guide the horses – they know the way. Back in the stable yard, each pair in turn goes to the drinking trough and, burying their noses deep in the water, draw in great draughts of it. When they have all finished, and before they are allowed into the stable, George whistles to them. A long-held quavering note repeated and repeated until, mares first and geldings after, they put their hind feet apart and stale. Only Ginger, who was

128

brought up in a town stable, never managed to perform to order, which is another thing George has against him. 'I don't mind hoss dung – and that you can't avoid – but hoss piss's different – that stinks, and besides it ain't good for a hoss to be standing in wet all night.' So, like children, they have been trained and brought up proper: clean in their habits. George detested Ginger, too, because he was inclined to get mange and suffered from greasy legs – ailments which can take up a lot of unpaid-for time. And Ginger, more than any other in the stables, was liable to 'Monday Morning Leg'. The first time I heard Willy say his horse had 'Monday Morning Leg' I thought it was a joke, but no, it is a recognized complaint, where one or both hind legs swell up while they are not being worked on Sunday. The way to avoid it is to cut down their oats on that day or any non-working day. But, if they do have it, the cure is light work and little feed, and recovery is quick.

I have said the Y.L. plough is an all-iron implement, but it did have two six-inch wooden sleeves round the iron handles, held by a collar in front and a nut on the threaded after-end. In time, these wooden sleeves split and were bound with twine or riveted through, but in the end they fell away and were replaced by two half-sleeves of wood or just a wrapping of old sacking material – very uncomfortable. Just before I went to Home Farm, an unhappy accident occurred with one of these handles. An old plough was standing on a headland; its wooden handles had fallen away and it was left with just a twist of sack round them. Moreover, the holding nut had gone and the thread had rusted into a thin spike. A neighbouring farmer exercising a greyhound much fancied for the Waterloo Cup, put up a hare on the field and slipped his dog after it. The hare ran across the field with the greyhound close behind, full speed past the plough and then turned sharply. The dog, in trying to follow the hare, ran full gallop into the plough handle, whose sharp point went into its chest and out at the shoulder. It hung there, and when the farmer came up to it it was dead. Sometimes I was told the farmer 'wouldn't have had that happen for a thousand pound'; sometimes the figure was five hundred or even a mere hundred; and with variations I heard the same story from every other man on the farm – but the manner of the dog's death was not varied.

I know it is puzzling to many people that the older countrymen take most pleasure in oft repeated tales. A new one is suspect; it has to be thought over and weighed up before it can be re-told without groping for words. The old ones come out easily – the teller can concentrate on building up the suspense, watching his listener's expression and judging nicely when to produce the culminating line. I once sat in the village pub and listened to five men tell the same story, one after the other. It was about a man with a footbridge over a ditch, which villagers persisted in using as a short cut through his property. Since suitable warnings to those concerned had no effect, he stole out one night and half-sawed through the planks of the bridge, knowing that the next person to cross would break through and be thrown into the water. Alas! next morning, forgetting what he had done, *he* walked on to the bridge himself and with proper justice fell through on to his back in three feet of dirty water. The first teller of the story told it chronologically starting with the background to the story and finishing with the man in the water. The others started at different points, emphasizing special angles – the time he took to saw through the bridge – the kind of (superior) clothes he was wearing when he fell – what he said as he fell – but at the end of each telling we all roared with laughter. There were two more men in the bar, and I was sorry they did not also give us a version – it would not have been too much.

Stories like this, where the high-and-mighty or the sneaky were taken down and their folly exposed, were favourites. The farmer who would spy through a knot-hole in the barn door at his men tried it on one day to find that a little bit of looking glass had been stuck over the hole, so all he could see was the reflection of his own mean eye. 'A'course he could'n say nothen, do we'd have ast him what he wanted to look through the hole for.' The same farmer, I was told, used to send his aged father to creep about the fields to watch what his men were up to. One day, as he crept down a ditch alongside where they were hoeing, he was spotted. Their leader passed the word round and at a signal they all hollered: 'Look out there, hey up, goo on! There goo a rabbit!' And they threw stones and hoes into the hedge in front of the ditch where the old man was crouching. When he got up, they asked him if the rabbit had got away. When he said he thought so, one suggested it had crept down *an old foxes' hole* – which witticism was repeated for weeks: 'You sh'd hev sin his face – the old fox!' Then there were stories of the 'I told him, but he wouldn't have it' kind – ones usually ending in disaster for the too clever by half or know-all boss.

131

The way of the agricultural innovator is thick with difficulties and is made heavy going by the weight of traditional caution − sometimes unfairly so. 'I say that 'ont work − he say that will − but I'll make damn sure that *don't*, then 'haps he'll b'lieve what I say is right!' Such obstructive tactics were not met with on our farms. The Guv'nor understood what was at the back of the traditions and was careful not to bring in any new scheme too quickly. Rather, as he would say when we were making a fuss, trying to get cattle or pigs into a place where they would prefer not to be − 'Let them draw,' he would say. 'Let them draw; they'll go if you give them time − just let them draw,' and, providing you stood blocking the alternative ways, that's what they did − they drew in.

Chapter Seventeen

THRESHING was a job I disliked. It is all right pitching the sheaves down from the heights of the stack roof, well above the drum, but this was a job I rarely got. Traditionally, the boy of the gang bags off the chaff and clears away the calder or cavings — we used both terms — from the bottom of the straw pitcher. This is the dusty end of operations. Engine drivers are a cunning race, and before old Alby drew his tackle between stacks he was careful to note the direction of the wind and place the engine so that the dust from the drum was blowing away from it. There was another reason for this, in that only a senior man had the job of taking off and weighing the corn, and he too liked to be out of the dust. So, against those two, what the rest of us thought didn't count for much.

The next dirtiest job to the chaff-boy's was that of feeder. He stood atop the drum, cut the twine round each sheaf as it came to him from the stack, and fed it into the machine. Again, he would be a senior man accustomed to the work, and not liable, as a boy might be, to slip down into the fast revolving drum. Dreadful tales are told of men who carelessly reached forward for a sheaf, or tripped and fell through the opening: limbs torn off, and death before a doctor could be called for. The straw stack was built by the head dayman; while the horsemen did the carting away of corn to the granary. The constant harsh hum of the drum, 'whumping' now and then when the feeder let a larger-than-usual sheaf fall in whole; the endless slap of belt fasteners on pulleys; the rumbling rhythm of the shakers and straw-walkers, these were bad enough – but the dust, the endless blast of gritty dust laden with sharp bits of straw, barley avels or the equally nasty oat flights, tormented me almost to mutiny. A very few men said they didn't mind the chaff-bagging job; but it was noticeable that it usually went to unimportant people who were in no position to complain.

Most threshing outfits travelling in an area were regularly followed by the same 'casual' men. 'Casuals', but experts of their kind, they became used to the engine driver and the ways of his machine, so at a pinch they could help out with a belt repair or clear a blocked sieve without having to be told how to do it. Occasionally these casuals had among their number one who would take off the chaff, but if so he would probably be a simpleton – stupid and incapable of anything less mechanical. In some places, when the threshing tackle arrived, the farmer would go round to the local boys' 'home', and hire some poor dim-witted orphan for a few shillings a day to do the dirty work. And the food they brought with them made our grub look like a feast – thick hunks of stale grey bread with a thin smear of dripping or maybe lard – and 'water from the hoss-trough if you're thirsty, boy'. The Guy'nor would not, I think, have had lads like these on the farm at any time (one wonders whether in fact their employment was legal), but in any case, while I was there, he had no need! Georgy and I were of an age, but he had already acquired skills which took him beyond the chaff-bag – so it fell to me.

134

I can remember the relief when a belt came off, or we stopped for the day: the way the feeder stopped feeding; how Alby raced up the engine to blow all the odd ends and dust from the drum and then slapped shut the throttle; how the governor balls slowed, the fly-wheel stopped, and the only sound was a faint escape of steam and men flapping dust from their jackets, rolling up the belts, and sheeting up the drum. That moment was bliss. It was the moment too for men to pull out their pipes – not to smoke, because this was against the stackyard rules – but to get them blown out and sweetened by a blast of steam from one of the exhaust pipes curling under the belly of the engine. You jammed the pipe-bowl tight against the vent, Alby opened a valve, and the steam jetted through the pipe, coming out of the mouthpiece thick at first and yellow with tar, and then white and clean – and the purifying operation was complete. This was a regular threshing-time routine, and certainly a pipe smoked very smoothly afterwards. Nowadays, if I hear a steam engine, or even a tractor-driven threshing drum, I feel a strong urge to be with it; so perhaps the pleasant recollection of the rhythm of the job, of the comradeship of men all working together in harmony to one end, in retrospect balances out the scarring memories of dust, dust and more dust. Incidentally, while threshing corn is bad enough, the dust from peas or beans is heavier and hangs thicker in the air – worse, perhaps, even than the dust from the clover huller – though that takes some beating, too.

Corn stacks were built in pairs, so that at threshing time the straw from two stacks would make one straw stack. The threshing tackle would stay in the same place for both – the feeder merely moving from one side of the drum platform to the other. So far as I know, our straw stacks were made by men only, but on several farms in the neighbourhood they used a horse to stamp the stack as well. It was a common practice all over East Anglia at one time, and I was told the horse soon got used to walking round and round, more or less up to its belly in yielding straw. This technique could only usefully be employed if the straw stack was going to be built at least to eaves' height in one day, because, although you can get a horse (with a bit of encouragement) to slide from a considerable height into a bed of loose straw, it would be quite impossible to get him up again next day. I have never inquired — perhaps they simply left the horse with a bucket of water and a bite of hay up on top all night? In any case, I fancy they wouldn't have used their best horses for the job.

Straw stacks were seldom thatched — they were hardly worth the expense — and I was glad of it, since it could have fallen to my lot to act as thatcher's mate, and I'd done my stint of that after harvest. Thatching is an interesting and skilled job: that of thatcher's mate is semi-skilled back-breaking, and if the straw you are 'yelming' is new, it is a hand-scouring operation too. Half a wagon-load of wheat straw at a time is brought to the yard. This has to be shaken out into a long narrow 'bed' - just lightly thrown into that shape with a fork. Then, with a pail from the three-wheeled water cart, it is soaked; the water is just thrown over it until it is wet through. That part is easy. You next 'pull' the straw — walking, bent double, pulling handfuls out from the long side of the bed and laying them in a line parallel to it. The weight of the wet straw holds the mass fairly tight; so, as the straw is drawn, it pulls out straight. When you have gone the whole length, you have a bed of drawn straw the same size, but only three or four inches deep. Then, the yelming process. Beginning at one end, and with legs straddling the drawn straw, you proceed elbows-out to 'paddle' it with the outer edge of your palm and fingers, moving forwards at the same time so as to straighten the straw further. That done, you put one hand on the middle of the bed and with your fingers comb out the ends you originally grasped to pull it from the wet bed. This removes the short and bent straws. At this stage the stuff is roughly in bunches, and these are picked up and put in the thatcher's yoke, to be carried up the ladder to him when he yells 'shoof!' Incidentally, the word sheaf was always spoken as *shoof* and the plural, sheaves, as *shoofs* – both in straw for thatching and corn in the sheaf. The trouble with me was, the thatcher always shouted 'shoof' before I had done yelming. It was the constant work with a back bent double I found so tiring, and, when 'old Phoebe' was shining overhead, it was sweating work, too.

'Old Phoebe' or 'Bright Phoebe' was a common expression. At harvest time it was 'Come on, old Phoebe, do the barley 'ont never git dry today', or 'Bright Phoebe's bin hid up all day; doubt that'll rain afore night'. I wondered how it was that this name for the sun came to be used so commonly – it was not even used in a particularly jocular fashion. And even today Suffolk men of my, and older, generations still use it sometimes without thinking. Did it come from some ballad sung in early Victorian times? – unlikely, I think. More possibly, it has been used here since the first Elizabeth, and if there is a bit of confusion between

137

Phoebus the sun and Phoebe the moon, well, this is Suffolk.

The thatcher was a little gnome of a man, but a demon for work. He scuttled up and down the ladder at tremendous speed, laying the yelms, knocking in the hazel broaches (we pronounced them *brorchers*; a thing which had me foxed when I was told off to go and cut a bundle, since I knew them by the Essex name of *springels*) faster than I could cope with. I can see him now, lying spreadeagled on the roof against the bright sky, placing, smoothing, combing and pushing the broaches in, shouting, 'Shoof! come on! do we 'ont niver git done.'

The Home Farm fences and hedges were tall, wide and overgrown, but rarely stockproof. The thorn and elm had grown leggy with age; horses and cattle in hungry times had eaten the lower branches, and then forced their way through in the hope of finding better grub next door, making gaps which we were always repairing with stakes and odd bits of baler wire or old pieces of barbed wire. I never saw a new roll of barbed wire the whole time I was there. Worst of all was the 'cow meadow' – the field where the cows spent most of their time. This had woods on two sides, an arable field on a third and the lane on the fourth. All of them were patched and wired, and none of them held cattle for long. One night – it would be in October or November, I think – the Guv'nor shouted me out of bed to help him round up the herd, which had got out and into the sugar beet next door, the field where I first hoed. This field was so large he thoughtfully brought the pony mare for me to ride, since the animals might

138

be anywhere on the field – or, indeed, beyond. No saddle, I jumped on her back and set off.

It was a night to remember. The day had been warm and there was a bright three-quarter moon shining on a dense carpet of mist five foot deep. The hedges stood above it, the tops of gate-posts jutted up, the stacks, their roofs illumined, their walls hugely black, swam in a white unmoving sea. Highly romantic – but making the search for cattle far from simple. I set off along the lane boundary, and saw and heard nothing. Then along the park woods, and still nothing. Then down the third headland, with the same result. The Guv'nor was waiting at the gate, and I reported. 'You'll have to "quarter" it then,' he said. 'Take a hundred-yard strip at a time – follow the beet rows and you won't get lost.' So off I went again, without realizing the Guv'nor had been pulling my leg about following the rows – since these were completely invisible.

However, after a few bewildering casts across the field, stopping and listening from time to time, a horned head suddenly broke the mist a few yards away. Good, I've found them! Looking closer, I discovered rather I had found *him* – the old bull. And I knew two things; although he was ordinarily quiet and good tempered, he did not like me and he hated horses. Only his head was visible: two dirty great down-turned horns with curly hair between, two eyes glinting meanly in the moonlight, and two jets of hot air steaming wide from his nostrils as he winded me and considered the situation.

I was doing some considering, too. The bull – his name was Tom – snorted, lowered his head and of course disappeared. I thought he was about to charge, and prepared to gallop for safety; but instead of charging Tom merely pawed the ground and bellowed. He pawed to such effect that he threw a whole series of sugar beet over his shoulder and then looked up to see if I had gone. Seeing me still in position, he lowered again and made a rush. But, of course, with his head down he couldn't see me any more than I could see him – so I listened, and moved off to mingle with the cows which had come up to see what was going on. Their heads stuck up above the mist like a lot of old aunts looking over the fence at something unseemly. I rode through them, got behind, and, yelling at them to go on home, drove them towards where I had last seen Tom. It worked. Once the cows started moving, the old bull took up the lead and took them quietly down towards the gate where the Guv'nor turned them back into their meadow. Apart from a few beet eaten and a few thrown out of the ground by Tom, no damage was done – though cattle in sugar beet is not a good thing: oxalic acid in the fresh green leaves can poison them, though when thoroughly wilted they are quite safe and, I think, more palatable.

Next morning the cowman filled the gap in the hedge, but a week later another escape sparked off a serious hedging programme. This time the cows got into the wood. They spent two or three happy hours browsing before they were missed and brought home for evening milking. Nothing seemed amiss. The milk was put in churns and trundled to the dairy, where it stood overnight ready for delivery next day. But when Georgy took the lid off for the house milk next morning, he found it stinking of onions. Sixty gallons of foul onion-flavoured milk. Actually, it was garlic; the woods there were thick with wild garlic, and the cows had eaten enough to taint their milk. Not only that night's milk, but the morning's, too, was the same – quite unsaleable. Madam tried skimming the cream, in the hope that butter churned from it would be all right. It wasn't – it, too, stunk – and in the end the lot went to the pigs and we went hedging. The Guv'nor couldn't afford another accident of that kind.

Bramble scythe, brushing hook and slasher were our hedging tools. The bramble scythe was a short, stout-bladed tool for cutting the long grass and nettles and straggling brambles from the brews in front of the hedge; the brushing hook for the same job on ditch sides where the scythe couldn't be swung; and the slasher for cutting the hedge itself. I'm afraid that here, as in the rest of Suffolk, there was no tradition of good

141

hedging, no layered fences with pleached tops. At best, they were 'buck topped' – just cut level and the sides trimmed; and, at worst, 'slopped' down to the ground with enough stout uprights left for stapling wire to. But, though it may have lacked art, it was pleasant work. In late summer, with growth at its full strength, the smells from crushed nettles and bruised leaves and the scent from cut hedge-stems tickled the nostrils. Each kind of fresh cut wood has its own smell. Mostly the differences are hardly definable, but the rank odour of elder, the kippery smell of oak, the acrid elm and the almost bland warm smell of field maple are distinctive. Smells have a way of embedding themselves deep in the unconscious: you forget them, you can rarely conjure them up in the way that you can recall sounds and tastes; and then, suddenly, some tiny whiff on the air and you are back vividly perhaps forty years to the time and place where you first knew it.

The smell of burning hedge takes me back to the Home Farm woodside hedge, and a bait time. We were sitting on the cleared bank, our bread and cheese finished, our tea bottles stuck upright in the grass ready for the last drink before getting back to work. Legs stretched out, pipes going, enjoying the mild sun, listening to the larks and the grasshoppers, and watching swallows gliding round our fire to catch smoke-bemused flies. Willy was arguing with Bob about the time when the hedge was last cut, an argument involving complicated calculations about what grew when and where. Willy held it must have been when the next field was last in to beans, and he worked his way back over the crops – fifteen years – to prove it. Bob made it longer than that – but, having been proved wrong for one crop year, his calculation was thought to be inaccurate. Later I asked the Guv'nor, and he knew, of course, because he carried in his head an exact picture of what each field had grown in the thirty years he had farmed there. In the event, neither Bob nor Willy was right – both had forgotten a second crop failure one year, which had put their calculations awry. The Guv'nor not only knew the exact cropping history of each of his own fields, but of the roadside fields of other farmers for miles round almost as well. As he drove he looked to right and left, peering over hedges and through gateways, noting the stacks – in fact, looking everywhere but at the road he was travelling. I don't know how many fields the whole estate had – maybe seventy or more – but multiply seventy fields by thirty years, and appreciate the feat of memory. George was almost as good and had a knack of remembering in addition just how many pecks of seed were sown on each field. It was sitting by that fire I first heard about the local fish manure scandal.

It was like this. A dealer well known to be a sharpish sort of fellow offered a farmer thirty tons of condemned fish – to be used, as he thought fit, either for pig food or manure. It was not an uncommon sort of offer: condemned foodstuffs – meat or fish – were often bought, and either fed or spread on the land. 'How much are you asking for it?' asked the farmer who had a lot of pigs. 'Three pound a ton,' says the dealer, 'and I reckon, if you pick it over a bit, most of it 'd go for hog grub.' – 'Yes, I know all about condemned fish,' says the farmer. 'Stinking stuff – poison half of them pigs as like as not, but see here, I'll make you an offer – pound a ton and you deliver, or ten bob and I'll collect.' To his surprise, the dealer accepted. Cash paid on the spot; instructions to collect quickly.

Next morning the farmer gathered all his men, and as many horses and wagons as he could spare from work or borrow from neighbours, and sent them off to the docks, telling them to hurry both ways. He told his pigman: 'Get the swill boiler going, boy. Keep the hogs hungry this morning, and we'll give 'em a feast tonight to make up for it.' Late that afternoon the wagons returned. To the farmer's surprise, as they came into the yard, the horsemen were riding the wagons instead of leading the horses. A good sign, he thought; for if they can sit that close it must mean the fish isn't too far gone. Nor were they holding their noses; they were laughing and joking as if they had had a pleasant day out. The farmer sniffed the air: nothing nasty . . . not even a suspicion of fish about it; that was suspicious in itself. He realized almost as soon as the wagons drew alongside how skilfully he had been done. Instead of tons of useful raw, but smelly, loose fish, what he'd bought was thirty tons of elderly tinned pilchards in tomato sauce.

'They tell me,' said Willy, 'when he see what he'd got, he danced up and down and swore terrible and give his head man the sack on the spot – reckoned that was *his* fault – said he should've come home and left them tins where they was.' Cooling down he changed his mind about firing his man, but was still left with the problem of how to make use of the fish. He had the men sorting the tins. They discarded obviously mis-shapen, swollen ones, and put the reasonable-looking ones in a heap beside the cake-crusher, with a view to squeezing the tins of their goodness, which could then be collected and fed to the hogs. Unfortunately for

144

him, the only tins which really 'gave' were the ones already under internal pressure. As the crusher bore down on them, they exploded, sending foul gobs of decaying fish and tomato sauce over the man feeding it and his mate who was turning the handle.

But the farmer was not a man to be beaten without a fight. The tins were loaded into tumbrils and spread over a small field in preparation for brussel sprouts. When they were spread, he sent a pair of horses in his heaviest ring roll, thinking to burst them and release good fertilizer for the crop. This didn't work. The roll merely pressed them into the ground, which gave the field a scintillating surface but did no good. In desperation, he then sent his men out armed with stout forks and picks to puncture the embedded tins. Within an hour he was near to having a strike on his hands. The men, splattered with filth, stinking, refused to go on. He was beaten, and, putting in the plough, buried the lot. Years after, the field (which happened to be a roadside one) still showed a scattering of rusted tins each spring when the cultivators went through. The farmer never quite lived it down.

Chapter Eighteen

THERE were scores of stories told at 'bait' times by the men or by the Guv'nor on our journeys to sales. I had no direct contact with dealers, of course, but tales about them served as a warning later, when buying and selling through dealers became a part of life. Generally, though, conversation with the men was related to the job we were doing. If it was threshing, then the stories would be about high yields, or of the terrible injuries to men who had carelessly fallen into the drum, or, walking too close to an unguarded pulley, had had first their coats and then their limbs torn from them – things which, because of safety legislation, can hardly happen today. During hedging and ditching, I learned of the tricks of daymen, who would carry a ferret to work in their pockets and do a little quiet rabbiting at the same time. A purse net over a bolt hole, a wide net across a ditch, slip the ferret down another hole and carry on with hook and slasher until a thin scream or a struggle from the net meant a rabbit half-way to the cooking pot. In the event of the master approaching, nets could quickly be pushed under a turf, the ferret pouched or sodded up in the hole, and the bunny covered with brushings.

Not much of this sly activity went on at the Home Farm – or, if it did, I was not aware of it. The men would probably have trusted me not to split on them, but might well have feared that in my innocence I might unwittingly have given the game away. There was poaching, of course: the long net – a hundred yards or more of fine mesh – was known to be used in the parish, and not all the efforts of keepers, who stuck tangling thorn branches over the stubbles, could stop it. I never at that time took part, or knew for sure who went in for such dark night work, but I was quietly shown one or two other useful poaching methods which came in handy later on and are tempting to tell of. It is a temptation to be resisted, since they are traditional, and well enough known by those who need to know them – and to encourage those who do not would be folly.

Keepers played only a small part in our life. The shooting was a syndicate; the keepers were not over-keen or over-paid; and, if rumour was true, they were probably more active with long net and silent air rifle than the farm chaps. On the whole, they were despised more than feared; disliked, anyway, and always mistrusted, since, though they were no different by birth or upbringing from the rest of the villagers, they had authority and licence to inform. Perhaps because of this they are not the most attractive people. Constant and often unthinking war against what they believe to be the enemies of the game bird seems to blunt their sensibilities, and they are often cruel beyond reason. Our keepers were not particularly wicked or vicious, but hatred for owls, stoats, weasels, hedgehogs, hawks and kestrels, not to mention jays and magpies, had made them anti-life, and lost them a sense of wonder and reverence for nature. Maybe I exaggerate; I would not have so described them when I was at Home Farm

– they were just interfering busybodies and sneaks, with whom one passed the time of day, exchanged words on the weather and left it at that.

It is odd, though, that keepers, who spend so much of their time alone, watching and listening in the solitude of the woods and fields, are almost notorious for their belief in old exploded country saws. Ours were sure hedgehogs milked sleeping cows and that horse-hairs dropped in a pond or a well turned into eels. And, of course, because they depended for their living on being able to get along with 'the gentry', and were professionally in perpetual hope and expectation of handsome tips, they became 'yes-men', agreeing with anyone who might drop them half a crown. But still, I spent instructive days with one of the keepers, and learned from him how to 'squeak' rabbits from burrows. This is done on an in-drawn breath with tight lips and is thought to sound enough like the mating cry of a rabbit to deceive. This may be so and it is no disproof that the same noise will draw rats and stoats and ferrets in the same way. Hearing an expert squeaker, even hares will change direction and come limping along to find out what it is all about and pay the penalty for their curiosity.

Hares were knocked over by the men when chance offered – sitting tight in their forms, they make an easy target for a long stick – but few were eaten. In fact, then or now, country people don't much like hares. 'Wouldn't thank ye for a hare, they're too bloody for me, too strong, thanks all the same.' Women seem to have an aversion to preparing them and I've heard it said that when they are skinned, they look too much like a baby or a cat for comfort. Nor were

148

rabbits popular. Even when meat was hard to come by, there was prejudice against them. This was probably because, on rabbit-infested land, we saw too many – and, hulking them for the market, got sick of the smell. There was also the question of disease. Long before myxomatosis, when a rabbit population got too large for its grazing grounds, they would suddenly start to die off. Their livers became diseased with spots a leprous yellow colour all over. Good enough for the town, but not for us. There was a well-held belief that townspeople will eat anything: they wouldn't know the difference between an old doe rabbit about to kindle, a milky doe, or a stringy three-year-old buck from a clean three-quarter grown youngster – the only kind we ever ate. This belief was put to the test during the war, when we used to send great hampers of rooks and jackdaws for sale in London. They made good money, and I've never eaten game pie away from home since.

After harvest, with a lot of barley on his hands, the Guv'nor increased the pigs on the farm; and, since the Home piggeries were already full, the breeding stock and some fatteners as well, were sent down to the Lodge Farm a mile from Home Farm. The house there was empty, and, there being no cottages attached or workers belonging to it, I was told off to look after them. It was a job which took a couple of hours night and morning. The Lodge had not been farmed as a separate holding for many years and with no resident the yard and buildings had dilapidated and become tumble-down, and so overgrown with elm-suckers and ivy and brambles you might walk through the yard without knowing any buildings were there at all.

149

Georgy and I spent a couple of days slashing ways through to doors, cutting a path from the meal-shed to the loose boxes where the pigs were to go, and blocking up holes in the walls and in the meadow-fences where the sows would run. Water, since the pump was broken, had to be brought up in the three-wheel water cart every morning – and this fell to me as well. I hated that water cart. I hate all three-wheel water carts. Their wheels wobble and squeak, their lids never fit, their hinges are rusted through, they have rust-holes in their

bottoms, and if they are fitted with taps these are rusted solid. On top of these disadvantages, they are impossible to fill or empty by pail without getting yourself wet to the waist, and if you try to back them in a cobbly and uneven yard they usually tip over and lose you half the water. Looking back, I seem to have spent years struggling with three-wheel water carts. Water for sheep, when the field they were folded in was frozen and the cart racks deep, hard, and impossible to traverse without water jetting from the top at each jerk. Water for the steam plough, usually at work on a field most distant from water supply; and water for the threshing engine set in a sea of well-churned mud. There is this, too: you can't *ride* on a water cart without getting a wet seat – perhaps it is this which has left me with a rooted dislike for them.

We mended the loose boxes as well as we could, using boards pulled from even more ancient structures, old nails pulled out and hammered straight, and, of course, baler wire. It was a hodge-podge job; and since the footings of the boxes were rotten – the bricks loose in the mortar, the wooden plates on them wet-rotten through – the chances of their holding pigs secure for long were not great. We put the smallest pigs in the worst of them, and the sows in the next best, reserving the strongest for the old boar, because, as Georgy said, 'If he git his snout under the bottom bricks, he'll hev the whole lot down afore brackfast.'

The boar was an elderly and extremely bad tempered Large White, with a reputation both for getting sows in pig and for smashing up his quarters. He was called Sammy, and was the only animal on the farm Georgy was nervous of. So was I; when not with the sows, he seemed to spend most of his time standing with his nose to a crack in the wall, champing and chopping his ugly jaws until the froth flew. Feeding him was a problem. We had solidly nailed up the bottom of the half-doors, fearing that the hinges would give way or the hasp fly off if he put his weight to it. His trough was just inside the door, and the grub had to be tipped into it over the door. This was fine when the trough was in position and the right way up; but Sammy either filled it with muck between feeds, or flicked it upside down and to the far side of the box well beyond reach – so that it had to be retrieved. For a week or so I had no trouble; armed with a broom or fork, I hopped over the door and placed the trough, having first distracted Sammy with the bribe of a few roots or a handful of corn thrown in the corner furthest from where I had to go. This worked splendidly, and having also spent more time than the Guv'nor would have approved of in scratching Sammy's back with the sharp end of a dung fork, I foolishly came to believe that he was not the villain he was painted. I felt we had come to an understanding. The sows and fatteners were no bother, either. With plenty of fresh grass to root about in, the old girls didn't bother trying the fences, and the fatteners, being well fed, were well content too.

It was part of my job to see that three days after a sow was weaned, she was led to the embraces of Sammy to be put in pig again. This was not easy, since the door facing the yard was nailed and the only other door was at the back of the pen – a heavy affair fastened on the outside, and reached only by walking round the whole range of loose-boxes. Naturally, by the time I had managed to drive a sow round and get the door open to let her in without at the same time letting him out, Sammy was usually in a state of some excitement. His champing and frothing accelerated, and his assaults on the fabric of the building made it shake and shudder. He knew even better than I did when a sow was ready for service: his keen nose sniffed at the passing air and detected the first signs – and until she came to him he was inclined to rage a bit.

However, as I have said, I had got accustomed to

him, and was thus taken off guard when one evening, while I was retrieving his trough from the wall away from the door, he suddenly rushed me. Up until a split second before, he had had his nose to the wall, smelling for a gilt which had come from Home Farm that day – and I suppose he was feeling an acute frustration. He whipped round and charged with a sound like the roaring of lions. My reactions in those days must have been pretty good, for I acted swiftly too. No question of hopping over the door, since he was coming from that direction; no question of getting the other door open, since it was fastened on the outside. No question, either, of keeping him at bay, since I had no pacifying argument likely to succeed against half-a-ton of furious hog.

There was a beam seven foot above ground spanning the box, and, galvanized by fear and adrenalin, I jumped towards and over the charging animal and got my arms round it. His snout just touched my boot, and before he could turn and go for my dangling legs I swung them round the beam too. So there I was, arms and legs clutching the beam, with my backside drooping much too near Master Sammy's snapping jaws – and, as I noticed with added agitation, his unpleasant and wickedly curving six-inch tusk. The other had been broken off some time before; but I scarcely counted this a mercy. The beam was a hefty one – over a foot square; had it been thinner, I might have managed to get on to it without lowering my legs – but, as it was, I couldn't – it was too thick; and, since to lower a leg would mean getting it ripped, I was stuck where I was. In fear, too, lest Sammy should manage to rear up and catch my lower end. He stood

153

underneath champing, coughing and roaring with rage – the champing sound being particularly suggestive. I hung on and hollered. 'Help!' I shouted. 'Heeeelp!' I did so wholeheartedly, since I happened to know no one was at the Lodge that day nor likely to be near, and it might be hours before I would be missed. By which time. . . .

Once or twice Sammy eased off and half moved towards the crack in the wall, through which no doubt the scent of the gilt was drifting; but when I made a move to improve my position, cautiously easing a leg, he whipped round and took up his guard again immediately below. Exactly how long I was stuck up there, I don't know; half an hour for sure, maybe an hour. Long enough for my head to feel it weighed a ton, and to wish my jacket pockets had less in them. I just weighed too much for my strength. My shouts for help were drying in my throat when Georgy stuck his head over the half door and took in the situation. 'Hold you on for a bit, time I get a sow round,' he called – and before I could tell him about the gilt, he had gone. However, born stockman that he was, Georgy spotted the animal, and within five minutes, during which I really thought I would have to let go, he had it round to the back door. The moment it opened, Sammy rushed out, Georgy dodged in, slammed shut the door, and I dropped.

As I sat there rubbing my arms to get the circulation going, Georgy told me how it was just by chance that he had come to the Lodge at all. He had been at work two fields away putting a fence in order, and, breaking the shaft of his hammer, came over to get the one we had been using for building repairs. Once in the yard,

154

he heard Sammy and looked to see what was wrong. It was a lesson to me. Never lower your guard with a boar. 'No, and not with a bull neither,' said Georgy. 'They'll be nice as pie today and termorrer, and then when you tu'n your back, they'll hev ye.' Unfortunately the lesson had to be learned all over again with respect to bulls; but that came later. (I don't count the bull in the sugar beet episode, since the danger then was not very real.) After I'd got to my feet, and the blood was moving in my hands and arms, we went round the back of the boxes – where Sammy was doing his stuff – to get him back into his box. He had been successful: his lust assuaged, he dismounted and stood looking as innocent of vice as an eight-foot-long boar can – which is not very. I opened the door, Georgy whacked him with a stout cudgel, and, as his after-end disappeared through it, I gave him a mean and meaning jab with the sharp prongs of a two-tine fork. He scarcely noticed it. Since then, I have seen for myself the truth of what Georgy told me about the habit boars have of always

going for legs. They prefer the inner leg and, starting below the knee, will slash upwards, carving a deep slice to the top of the thigh as quick as lightning – and unless the unfortunate victim can get out and away, a few more slashes soon put him beyond human help. Their strength is colossal and the power of their jaws beyond belief. I have always liked pigs and do still, but I wasn't sorry to be shifted from the Lodge job soon after: Sammy would champ and froth so, and the memory of that long hang from the beam needed no refreshment.

I very rarely went to the Lodge; in fact, apart from the pig-feeding time, I can remember only one other occasion. This was earlier – in May, probably, when we had a young mare down there for foaling. She had been kept on light work up to a month or so before she was due, and then put on a little meadow (the same one we turned the sows on later) until she should be showing signs of being within a day or two of her time. This had arrived, and she was now in a big loose-box. George looked at her several times in the day, but late in the evening asked me to go down and see how she was faring. I opened the door and went in. Yes, she had started: the water bag was showing and within a few minutes the foal would be born. My instructions were to report back at once if she had started; so off I went to find George. Why, I don't remember, but he had gone off in an unexpected direction, and it was half an hour before I found and returned to the Lodge with him.

The mare was looking over the top of the door, which was strange, and – stranger – she seemed quiet and not at all worried. George went in, looked round the dark box and came out again. 'Are you sure you see the water bag?' I answered 'yes'. 'Well, tha's a rum un,

156

'cos there ain't no bag showen nor no foal neither,' and he turned away. But then he turned back. 'Suthen not right – that wholly smell like she've foaled,' and in he went once more. 'Here, mate – come you in here and look at this,' he called. I followed and found him standing over in the dark of one corner – looking not at the floor, but at the high manger and in it the foal. It was alive, but not kicking. We lifted it out all slippery and wet and, putting it on the ground, rubbed it vigorously all over with dry straw. After a few moments, the mare came over and joined in with her tongue, and within another few moments the foal was on its feet and sucking. I fancy George was annoyed at having been fooled. Perhaps he didn't believe I had seen the water bag in the first place, and found too easy confirmation in the absence of a foal on the floor. Anyway, he blamed himself: 'Should've known Blossom 'd foal ockard – har mother was jest the same – never did nothen' right . . . I orter thought about the manger, 'cos we've had that happen afore.' In fact, it was quite a common happening, and even my relatively limited experience of foalings includes two of foals dropped in mangers. And they were unnoticed for some time too.

Matchett, another mare, foaled a day later. They had been worked as a pair for the last weeks by George or Willy. Just light work in chains – harrowing and the like – and allowed to go their own pace, with frequent stops even in mid-field for staling, and plenty of time at each headland. This was the rule for in-foal mares: no weight on their backs for the last three months at least – which meant no carting – but as much gentle walking in a short day as they could comfortably take. The

157

Guv'nor, I think, was torn between pride in good foals and the loss of working time from the mares, but George and Willy enjoyed it with a single mind. For them, it meant a slight easing of work and, at the end, two new horses on which to exercise their skill – and possible replacements for aged or less good animals already in the stable. For me it was sheer pleasure. Is there anything nobler than a cart mare heavy in foal, belly richly rounded, coat shining over taut skin? I didn't think so – I still don't – unless it is when she and her week old foal are in a meadow like the one at the Lodge among green grass, high hedges, and with great oaks and elms for deep shade – the mare grazing, the foal with its head in her flank or looking out prick-eared and bright-eyed on this strange new world.

I was away when, months later, the colt foal (Matchett had a colt and Blossom a filly) was castrated. It was done by a man who travelled round the country cutting colts, bull calves and pigs. He wasn't a vet, but over the years he had acquired a reputation for the work and had some skill in veterinary matters beyond it. Suffolk was thick with men of this kind: without academic qualifications, but not without a rough-and-ready knowledge of animal ailments and old-fashioned remedies for their cure. After the war, those who were currently practising were registered and allowed to carry on, but unqualified newcomers were barred. Georgy cut all the pigs on the estate – a job which most pigmen do as well, though not often so quickly, as a vet can. The shepherd, too, was his own vet in this matter, though the method he used up until a year or so before my time, learned from his father and antique in the extreme, does not seem to commend itself to the modern farmer, or his shepherd. He simply cut the lamb's purse and then bit the spermatic cord, removing the testicles with his teeth. This sounds, and is I suppose moderately revolting, but it may be based on good surgical theory. Without the means for sterilizing a knife between lambs, infection could be spread; teeth were cleaner. It was a standard joke among the men that one of the questions a farmer would ask before he engaged a new shepherd was whether he had a full mouth. This was a *double entendre*. A 'full mouth' ewe is a ewe in her prime and not old enough to have lost teeth; a 'full-mouthed' shepherd would presumably be better equipped for his surgical tasks than one whose teeth were wobbly or absent.

It was in the best traditions of the relationship between farmer and shepherd that the Guv'nor never gave his man a direct order. He would suggest the ewes might do well on the eddish of a hay crop or the trimmings and odd plants from a harvested cabbage field, but he would not order him to take his sheep anywhere. There was an understanding between them, which still allowed room for each to believe himself in the right whatever happened – a most satisfactory arrangement. I had a little to do with the sheep – part of the Guv'nor's policy for me to see everything – carting odd jags of hay, or helping to cart hurdles, stakes, wire and water – since the flock was Suffolks and spent most of their time folded, except after harvest, when Shepherd led them to the barley stubbles. I say led, and this is what he did. Crook in hand, he walked ahead of the flock, one dog at his heels, the other bringing up the rear, and in this fashion would take them past ungated fields of

159

succulent greens with scarcely a glance behind. He had them trained; but he told me it was really a matter of getting one or two old ewes determined to follow him, and the rest would follow. These old ewes he made a fuss of, carrying bits of linseed cake or a sweet turnip in his bag for them – cupboard love.

With guidance from the Guv'nor the shepherd was a law unto himself. He worked where he wanted and the hours he wished, asked for and got the help he needed and went his own solitary way. Most shepherds with a flock of his size would have had a page – a regular boy to help setting out folds and with all the semi-skilled work while he learned the trade. But with the Guv'nor this was not so. Anyone might be told off for the job. I spent hours making folds: thumping holes in hard ground with a fold-pritch for the hurdle stakes, stringing up sheep netting, and in the season preparing the lambing yard in a dry meadow at Pantons. Here, we created a sort of hutment made of baled straw: a circular encampment forty yards across whose outer walls were made up of individual ewe-size pens roofed over with thatched hurdles, snug and warm against the winds.

That year the lamb drop was good; I did a night or two with Shepherd helping with difficult deliveries, carrying the iodine bottle to soak the newly severed navels and so avert navel – or joint-ill – an infection which kills. We took it in turns to go out every fifteen minutes and walk round the maternity wards, hurricane lamp in hand, to see that all was well, and then back to the drowsy frowsty warmth of the oil-stove-heated shepherd's hut. It had no windows – just a door and a ventilator on the back wall, and the whole affair was on wheels, so it could be shifted from season to season.

160

One thing the Guv'nor was emphatic about in connection with the hut, and that was that the ventilator must never be closed — 'no, and don't you stuff your hat into it, neither'! Too many shepherds coming out of the bitter cold on a winter's night have turned up the stove, blocked off all the fresh air, and, assisted by a drink from the spirits' bottle, have slept and died in their sleep from carbon monoxide poisoning. Every year almost, deaths from this cause were reported, and the Guv'nor wanted to be sure we didn't go that way too. So we angled the hut so that the prevailing winds at least didn't blow straight through the holes, and casually hung a coat to deflect what draughts might stray in.

With a second hurricane lamp hung in the middle, a rough plank bed covered with old coats on one side and an upturned box on the other, and the stove and pipes going full blast, it was warm and matey, and we lounged between duties and talked of sheep and lambing times and shepherds' lore. Most of it is now forgotten, but it was compounded of quite scientific up-to-date knowledge with inherited observations and new ones and a great many old saws: a rich mixture somehow typical of the stockman of those times. Shepherd heard my story of the college mutton episode with the remark, 'That chap never knew his job — damn fule, I sh'd say — he wa'nt fit not to be in charge of ship at all.' Unlike me, he enjoyed mutton, and regarded his perks, the lambs' tails, as a particular delicacy. Properly, the farmer should get half of these and the shepherd half, but Madam didn't fancy them; so to this day it is a dish I have never tasted. The men, of course, made fun of my acting as shepherd's page. Most jokes about sheep and shepherds are coarse, and those concerning the page very much so. If the lamb crop turns out extra good, with a high proportion of twins, the chaps would twit the shepherd, telling him his page had done his work well. As Walter said, 'There ain't nothen like a vig'rous randy young tup for getten lams.' And if the drop was poor, 'Guv'nor say he'll ha' ter git a fresh page for ye next tuppen time, Shepherd.'

Lambing was hard work: up all night with at most a cat-nap or two, and not much let up during the daytime; but at least we had water and hay carted for us, and a few roots to throw to the sheep. For me, this experience of lambing, like so many first experiences, had a double pleasure. The pleasure of observing wonderful things for the first time; and the pleasure of having taken part in them and become so accustomed to what was happening that, instead of exclaiming with surprise and happiness, I could treasure and hug it to myself and present an unconcerned face to the men about me. That I never quite succeeded was not for want of trying!

My time at Home Farm had never been fixed, nor did it ever occur to me to consider what I should do when the time for leaving should come. The days — good ones with horses, bad ones in the dust of the threshing drum — came and went. Season followed season, until a whole year had passed and it was coming Spring again. It had not all been without friction. On occasions I had irritated the men by my lack of know-how and clumsiness; and the Guv'nor perhaps justifiably felt I had identified myself too closely with the men: there was a conflict of loyalties. These difficulties were inevitable, and if anything it was remarkable, and a tribute to the

Guv'nor and the family, that they never led to more than a short-lived rise in household temperature.

But the break had to come. We had a row. A dozen dry cows at Pantons broke through a fence I had mended and got into a field of young wheat, and the Guv'nor was furious. For my part, I felt his railing to be unjust, since the fence needed more time and materials than he'd allowed me. He said hard things, and I expect I replied with lame excuses and – seeing no other way out of the immediate trouble – said I was going. Without another word, the Guv'nor turned on his heel, got in his motor and drove away.

I walked the mile back to the Home Farm, feeling alternately sorry for myself and angry at the injustice. I went slowly, round by the road, slashing at hedge-plants, not looking to where the men were, not answering their greetings. Through the front door, up the stairs and into my room. Toothbrush, shaving things, two shirts, a pair of shoes, a best suit, one tie, a couple of handkerchiefs, jammed into the old black gladstone, and I was packed. Then downstairs for my mac hanging behind the dairy door and a good-bye to Madam, who took my hand and said she was sorry I was going. By now, so was I – and Georgy, who, sensing something was up, had drifted round to the door, made it worse. 'He'll a cooled off b' mornen, doubt he 'ont say nothen' more – do you goo on back an' ax him should you go or stay? Reckon he'll say stay.'

But it was too late. The bit, feeble though it was, was between my teeth; and with the mac over my shoulder and the gladstone in one hand and a holly-stick in the other, I left. Farewell to Georgy, through the yard, up the lane past the cottages, round the bend and out on to the main road. My Home Farm days were done.

Farming Press Books & Videos

We publish a wide range of agricultural and veterinary books and videos. For more information or for a free illustrated catalogue of all our publications please contact:

Farming Press Books & Videos, Wharfedale Road
Ipswich IP1 4LG, United Kingdom
Telephone (0473) 241122   Fax (0473) 240501

The Spacious Days   Michael Twist

Growing up on a Buckinghamshire estate in the 1930s. Anecdotes about the farm staff, agricultural work, gamekeeping and the countryside.

On the Smell of an Oily Rag   John Cherrington

The classic account of a farming life. Includes early days in New Zealand and Patagonia.

The Horse in Husbandry   Jonathan Brown

A profusely illustrated account of how horses were managed on farms from 1890 to 1950.

Harnessed to the Plough (VHS Video)
Roger & Cheryl Clark with Paul Heiney

Roger and Cheryl Clark demonstrate a year of contemporary horse-drawn cultivations and harvesting on their Suffolk farm. Additional commentary by Paul Heiney.

Buttercup Jill   Peggy Grayson

Amusing and entertaining memories of a rural childhood just before World War II. Full of lively dogs, unpredictable horses and eccentric country characters.

The Hired Lad   Ian Thomson

A young man's first work on a Scottish farm when horses were yielding to the tractor and bothy life was rough and ready.

Farming through the Ages   Robert Trow-Smith

From earliest times to World War II, an account of Britain's farming history built around a remarkable collection of pictures.

Farming Press Books & Videos is part of the Morgan-Grampian Farming Press Group which publishes a range of farming magazines: *Arable Farming, Dairy Farmer, Farming News, Pig Farming, What's New in Farming*. For a specimen copy of any of these please contact the address above.